The

CUPCAKE DIARIES

The CUPCAKE DIARIES

Recipes and Memories from the Sisters of

GEORGETOWN CUPCAKE

Katherine Kallinis & Sophie Kallinis LaMontagne

Stars of the TLC Series *DC Cupcakes*

HarperOne
An Imprint of HarperCollins Publishers

HarperOne

HarperCollins books may be purchased for educational, business, or sales promotional use. For information please write: Special Markets Department, HarperCollins Publishers, 10 East 53rd Street, New York, NY 10022.

HarperCollins website: http://www.harpercollins.com

HarperCollins®, 🏭 ®, and HarperOne™ are trademarks of HarperCollins Publishers.

TLC, DC Cupcakes, and the TLC logo are trademarks of Discovery Communications, LLC, used under license. All rights reserved. *tlc.com*

FIRST EDITION

Designed by Jessica Shatan Heslin/Studio Shatan, Inc.

Library of Congress Cataloging-in-Publication Data

Kallinis, Katherine.
  The cupcake diaries : recipes and memories from the sisters of
Georgetown Cupcake / Katherine Kallinis and Sophie Kallinis LaMontagne. —
1st ed.
    p. cm.
  ISBN 978–0–06–209060–7
 1. Cupcakes. 2. Georgetown Cupcake (Bakery) 3. Kallinis,
Katherine—Diaries. 4. LaMontagne, Sophie Kallinis—Diaries. 5. Cookbooks.
I. LaMontagne, Sophie Kallinis. II. Title.
  TX771.K35   2011
  641.8'653—dc23   2011018108

11 12 13 14 15 SCP 10 9 8 7 6 5

To our grandmother Babee,
who inspired us to follow our dreams.
This is for you.

This book would not have been possible without the love, support, and hard work of so many individuals.

First and foremost, we would like to thank our grandparents Babee and Papou. Babee taught us everything we know about baking, and each day at Georgetown Cupcake, we are surrounded by reminders of her impact on our lives. We know you are watching over us, and we hope we've made you proud.

Since we first decided to open Georgetown Cupcake, our parents have been our biggest fans. Our mother, Mommy, was also our first "employee." You came on our opening day and ended up staying forever! We love you. We would also like to thank our father for his love and unfailing encouragement. You taught us the meaning of hard work and the joy of working for oneself. We love you too.

Our husbands, Ben Berman and Steve LaMontagne, have been by our sides every step along the way, waking up with us early every morning, staying up late with us every night, and keeping us sane. Thank you for loving us, supporting us, and believing in us. We love you both.

This book came together because of the outstanding efforts of our team at Harper-One and HarperCollins, and in particular, our wonderful and extremely talented editor, Jeanette Perez, whose vision for this book and positive energy and expert eye kept us on task. Thank you to Suzanne Wickham, Terri Leonard, Katy Renz, Suzanne

Quist, and the entire team at HarperOne for their amazing efforts and who played a crucial role in getting this book published so quickly!

Sheryl Berk, our wonderful collaborator, and her daughter and "cupcake expert" Carrie, were instrumental in helping us organize our thoughts and translate our memories into what you see on these pages. Thank you for all of your help, advice, encouragement, and positive energy. We couldn't have done it without you!

Thank you to our literary agent, Claudia Cross, at Sterling Lord Literistic, for believing in us from the very beginning, for sharing and believing in our vision for this book, and for making this book a reality.

To our agents at the Creative Artists Agency, Lisa Shotland and Ashley Davis, for believing in us and supporting us—thank you so much for all of your help in making this book happen!

Our photographer, Dayna Smith of ImageSmith Media, put in many long days shooting countless photos of our cupcakes and family recipes with the most beautiful results. Thank you for putting up with our crazy antics during our marathon cupcake photo shoots and for allowing us to take over your kitchen—unleashing our cupcake tornadoes—so many times! Your artistic talent was a crucial part of bringing our cupcakes to life on these pages. Thank you so much for your beautiful photography!

We also celebrate this book with our entire *DC Cupcakes* family. Filming *DC Cupcakes* has been such an amazing experience for both of us, and we couldn't have done it without the support and encouragement and effort of so many people at Big-Fish Entertainment and TLC and Discovery Communications.

Our executive producers at BigFish Entertainment, Doug DePriest and Dan Cesareo—thank you for believing in and taking a chance on us. Executive producer Mark Finkelpearl—thank you also for believing in us and for your passion and vision for this show from the very early days. And our dear friend and executive producer Terence Noonan, who walked into our bakery in the summer of 2008, saw something there and has been our biggest cheerleader along this journey. Thank you all for your passion and hard work and dedication in bringing *DC Cupcakes* to life.

The entire team at TLC and Discovery Communications has been an absolute joy to work with, including our director of production, Caroline Perez; SVPs of development and production, Howard Lee and Nancy Daniels; group president, Discovery and TLC Networks, Eileen O'Neill; TLC general manager, Amy Winter; group COO, Discovery and TLC Networks, Edward Sabin; VP of talent management and strategy, Jennifer Williams; director of talent management and strategy, Tara Patten; EVP of communications, Laurie Goldberg; director of communications, Shannon Martin; VP of marketing/branded entertainment, Michelle Theisen; SVP of marketing, Tom Carr; SVP of marketing Lara Richardson; director of marketing, Rose Stark; director of licensing John Paul Stoops; director of licensing Sue Perez-Jackson; and last but not least, CEO of Discovery Communications, David Zaslav. Thank you for believing in us and sharing our story with your viewers. We are very proud to be a part of the Discovery and TLC family.

Our staff at Georgetown Cupcake—thank you so much for your amazing hard work, every single day. Your dedication, passion, and smiles are what help make Georgetown Cupcake the magical place that it is, and we couldn't have done this without all of you. Thank you for everything you do.

Finally, we would like to thank our customers and the fans of *DC Cupcakes* all across the country and the world. We quit our jobs to open Georgetown Cupcake because we had a dream to open a bakery together and because we wanted to share our grandmother's recipes, and her spirit, with everyone around us. We are so touched by all our fans who come to Georgetown Cupcake not just to try our cupcakes, but also to experience the magic of our bakery and share with us their own personal family stories and special moments and to talk with us about their own dreams. We hope that the memories and recipes in this book provide additional inspiration, encouragement, and enjoyment to everyone chasing their dreams. This is for all of you.

CONTENTS

INTRODUCTION

····································

The Grand Opening of Georgetown Cupcake

We had been waiting for years for this day to come, and to say we had butterflies fluttering in our stomachs is putting it mildly. Technically, we'd been dreaming of this day since we were young girls baking cupcakes in our grandma Babee's kitchen in Hamilton, Ontario. Everything we learned about baking we learned from her. We would stand beside her at the kitchen counter as she worked her magic. We remember her in her royal blue dress with large white polka dots and one of her many Greek aprons with beautiful flower embroidery lining its edges, her hair tied back in a white kerchief. She taught us how to cream butter and sugar together to make cakes and how to properly knead dough to make bread. We watched her, mesmerized.

Babee passed away at the age of eighty-two, when we were in high school. We miss her every day, and we realize now what a wonderful gift she gave us. Not just cherished memories and delicious recipes, but an absolute *passion* for baking. How much

1

Clockwise from top left: Babee; Babee *(second from left)* and Mommy *(far right)* with Babee's sister-in-law *(far left)* and sister; Sophie *(left)* and Katherine; Katherine *(left)* and Sophie

of a passion? Well, we gave up our steady and stable jobs in fashion and finance to open a bakery! It took us two years to make up our minds to go for it (a lot of people told us we were crazy!) and six months to sign a lease on a tiny-yet-charming town house tucked away on a side street in one of Washington, DC's most historic neighborhoods.

But now the day was here, and we looked at each other, in our flour-covered aprons, in ecstatic disbelief. After replacing the old, uneven floors with shiny-new birch planks; painting the walls a clean, bright white; installing our countertops and worktables; setting up our kitchen equipment; and hanging our menu on the wall, we were down to our last dollar. We needed to open as soon as possible. With no time or money to do any advertising, we splurged on a small sign that said, "GRAND OPENING VALENTINE'S DAY!" and hung it in our shop's large picture window a couple days before.

> *We realize now what a wonderful gift Babee gave us: an absolute passion for baking.*

Now, as we watched the digital oven timer count down on our very first batch of Red Velvet cupcakes, it suddenly all became real. Surrounded by the intoxicating aroma of fresh buttercream and chocolate wafting in the air and the hypnotizing buzz of our twenty-quart stand mixer whipping up clouds of vanilla cream-cheese frosting, it hit us: this was our livelihood. The only question was . . . would anyone show up?

The two of us and our mother, "Mommy" (as we love to call her!), arrived at the shop that morning at four to start baking. It was cold and dark outside, and while the rest of the city was fast asleep, we quietly switched on the lights in our kitchen, put on our aprons, and turned on the ovens for our first day in business. Mommy always volunteered to help us with whatever we were doing. We knew her kitchen skills were a little lacking, but we weren't about to turn down an extra pair of hands and a great cheerleader. As we methodically set out all of our ingredients to get started, we wondered aloud to one another what today would be like: how many customers (if any) would come in? What would be the most popular cupcakes? Would people *like* what we baked? We worked together as a team and started with our Chocolate cupcakes: we creamed the butter and sugar, added the eggs, mixed slowly and carefully before

Now the day was here, and we looked at each other, in our flour-covered aprons, in ecstatic disbelief.

adding the sifted flour and baking soda, then finally milk, vanilla, and cocoa powder. We lined cupcake pan after cupcake pan with delicate brown baking cups, scooped in the batter, and placed the first pans in the oven. Soon we had developed a rhythm and moved on to our Red Velvet cupcakes, and then the Vanilla. The smell of the warm cupcakes coming out of the oven floated through our entire building and out the windows. It took a lot of self-control not to eat them!

All the while, we kept our eyes on the clock, watching the hours fly by, and by eight, the two of us and Mommy had baked five hundred cupcakes, all lined up perfectly on brand-new shining sheet pans, ready to be frosted. As the cupcakes cooled, we quickly whipped up our signature vanilla cream-cheese frosting and melted down Callebaut chocolate chips and heavy cream to make a rich, piping-hot chocolate ganache.

When we came up from the kitchen to start frosting the cupcakes, our excitement slowly gave way to panic. As we peered out the front window, we could see a line starting to form . . . when we didn't open for another hour! Under the watchful eyes of what would become our very first customers, we went about our tasks at a frenzied pace: frosting the cupcakes with our signature swirl; dipping our chocolate cupcakes in bowls of glossy melted chocolate and covering them with crunchy toasted hazelnuts; folding boxes to store behind the counter; brewing pots of coffee; and placing

a vase of fresh flowers on the lone table at the front of our shop. All the while, we watched that line; now fifteen minutes before opening, it snaked all the way down the block! By 10:00 A.M., we had decorated our five hundred cupcakes and were ready to go. Earlier this morning, we thought that if we sold that many cupcakes, the day would be a huge success. As we turned on the lights to our shop and prepared ourselves to open the door, we wondered, would five hundred be enough?

They weren't. The first two hours of Georgetown Cupcake were a tornado of activity. We worked the registers, packed cupcakes, made lattés, answered the phones, and gift wrapped more boxes than we thought was possible. As the clock struck noon, we looked at our cupcake racks and were stunned at what we saw—there was nothing left! What we thought would be a day's supply had vanished in two short hours. Wondering how we would explain to customers that we had run out of cupcakes on Valentine's Day, we did the only thing we could do: We posted a note on the door saying that we were temporarily sold out and that we would reopen later in the afternoon with fresh cupcakes.

As the three of us stumbled back downstairs to our kitchen, we struggled to come up with a plan of attack. We had to reopen as soon as possible, but we also had to have cupcakes ready to sell. We frantically baked another three hundred cupcakes, fighting every impulse to rush. As any baker will tell you, you can't rush through the process of baking. You can't eyeball your ingredient ratios, you can't overbeat the cake batter, and you can't remove the cupcakes from the oven before the timer counts down to zero. As we continued baking, one of us would periodically sneak upstairs to peek out the window. The line was back, and it had grown even longer than before. Every second on our oven timer now seemed like an eternity. Moreover, we were running low on ingredients. Just as we feared, we quickly emptied the last sacks of flour; whatever we baked would have to carry us for the rest of the day.

Our faces streaked with cocoa powder and our aprons covered in batter, we reopened at 4:00 P.M. with three hundred fresh cupcakes, and the tidal wave of customers swept through our store once more. This batch ended up lasting another two hours, and as we pulled the last few cupcakes from our racks, we could see the worry start to settle on the faces of some of our customers in line. Would there be enough? Or would the person in front of them be the one to walk away with the last gift-wrapped Red Velvet?

In the end, we had to turn some customers away with the promise of fresh cupcakes the following day. There was simply no way we could shut down, rebake, and open again that day. As we closed the door to the shop and turned out the lights, we were mentally and physically exhausted. Most of all, we were in shock. We couldn't wrap our heads around what had just happened. We looked at one another, half thrilled and half terrified. And then we looked around our shop, at the empty coffee cups lining the counter, the dirty mixing bowls in our dish sink, and the sugar- and flour-covered floors and counters. All we wanted to do was sleep, when the reality of our business hit us again—sleep was no longer an option.

FEBRUARY 14, 2011

Three years later, the memory of that first Valentine's Day at Georgetown Cupcake seems like a lifetime ago. We've since moved from our tiny shop on Potomac Street into a larger store a block away and hired more than two hundred full- and part-time staff. And we now bake ten thousand cupcakes each day at our Georgetown shop and have come up with over eighty different flavors (see page 220 for the entire list). We have people coming to our bakery from all over the world just to try our cupcakes. We have baked on TV with both Martha Stewart and Oprah. And in 2009, the TLC

Network discovered our little bakery and decided to showcase our crazy lives in a television series called *DC Cupcakes*. Sometimes we have to pinch ourselves to make sure this is all really happening!

How did we get here? As we said, it started with our passion. When we opened Georgetown Cupcake, we were determined to make the best cupcakes in the world—to use the very best ingredients; to bake our cupcakes fresh throughout the day, every day; and to make them taste amazing. We believe that cupcakes are more than just delicious little treats, and there's a reason they're perennial favorites. They are a reminder of your childhood, of parties with friends, of playdates, of sweetness and sunshine and pure joy. They allow you to indulge, yet not *over*indulge. They are individual, little pieces of edible art that capture your personality and speak to your soul.

When we baked with Babee, there was a certain satisfaction in knowing that something we made by hand could make others in our family happy. And that's what we wanted to do with our Georgetown Cupcakes: make people happy. An added plus: *we're* happy just working together in our bakery every day. Some people can't imagine working *one* day with their sister, but for us it's a blessing. We know that we'll always be there for

each other, no matter what. We've come a long way, and we still love what we do. While our bakery is often fast-paced and chaotic, we find a certain peace in being there together. And we know in our hearts that Babee is proud of us.

This book is our diary of our dream; how it began, where it led us, and where we dream about going tomorrow. Within each monthly entry, we share our favorite baking memories from childhood and from our lives at Georgetown Cupcake. And in the final chapter, we talk about what it's like to film a television show and reveal some of the behind-the-scenes secrets from the set of *DC Cupcakes* (you won't believe some of the crazy things that happen!). And of course, we're delighted to share many of our favorite cupcake and dessert recipes so that you can make them in your own home.

We hope that these diaries inspire you to bake and moreover to celebrate baking as a way to bring family together. Most of all, we hope this book inspires you to take a leap of faith and follow and live your dreams, whatever they may be.

Sophie and *Katherine*

Recipe for Success

Always Challenge Yourself to Do Your Best

By the time we got to the fall of our first year—almost seven months after we had opened our doors—we thought we could relax a little. We'd found our groove, hired more staff, and just gotten through our first spring and summer alive. It seemed we were finally on cruise control and could relax a little. But then came a surprise . . .

The Washington Post announced they were launching a "Cupcake Wars" competition to rank all the cupcakes in the city. They were going to review two bakeries each week, and then do a final showdown to crown the city's best cupcake. When we heard about this, we knew that we had to win. Losing was not an option. We felt a tremendous amount of pressure. We had started the bakery, in part, to be able to work together, have fun, and do what we loved. Now, out of the blue, we were going to be judged in a serious competition by serious food critics. We were freaking out! So we gathered our staff and said, "It's all hands on deck—everyone needs to be on their A-game!" The most stressful part was that the editors were coming in undercover, and we had no idea when they would arrive or what flavors they would purchase.

We knew we had a strong cupcake lineup and had just unveiled our Caramel Apple cupcake (see recipe, page 18)—a fresh apple cupcake, cored and filled with a creamy caramel center, a vanilla cream-cheese frosting, and a drizzle of caramel sauce. So we felt confident, but we were still a bucket of nerves. What if they didn't like the cupcakes? We made sure that each and every cupcake leaving the shop was absolutely perfect, something that we still do to this day. Each Wednesday morning that month, we would eagerly open up *The Washington Post* and flip to the food section, just waiting for our judgment day. We read every week, as a competing bakery would get a scathing review and a paltry two out of ten, even a zero out of ten! We were terrified. The food editors were not holding anything back!

And then came the day. We opened the paper and there it was. Georgetown Cupcake! We took a deep breath and read what the reviewers had to say. The food editor said that our cupcakes were the Nadia Comaneci of the cupcake world: "Cute, small, and the first to score perfect 10s!" We had gotten an average of 9.8 out of 10 . . . a nearly perfect score that crushed every other bakery in the competition! At the end of the finals, not only did we win *best* cupcake with our Chocolate Ganache, our other flavors won the top seven of the top-ten spots. We were ecstatic! We jumped up and down and screamed! We *really* screamed! We were *so* happy—and most of all, relieved! We had just survived our first major review. For any young business owner, this is a huge milestone. It was an amazing feeling and pumped us up for the rest of the fall. We felt like we were ready for anything, and all we had done was our very, very best, sticking to our goal of making each and every cupcake perfect. The critic appreciated it, our customers appreciated it, and it taught us never to rest on our laurels and to raise the bar every day for ourselves.

sisters' baking secret

We love how baking lets our creative minds run wild. But when it comes to measuring ingredients, precision is the key. Here's a handy list of conversions to help you out with the recipes in the book and while shopping in your local grocery store.

1 pound = 16 ounces
1 cup = 8 ounces or ½ pound
½ cup = 4 ounces or ¼ pound
¼ cup = 2 ounces or ⅛ pound or 4 tablespoons
1 tablespoon = ½ ounce
1 teaspoon = ⅙ ounce
pinch = ¼ teaspoon
1 stick butter = 4 ounces or ¼ pound or 8 tablespoons

Part 1

AUTUMN

Autumn is one of our favorite seasons. The air becomes cool and crisp, and the leaves turn a magical array of rainbow hues. We love this time of year because it means pulling our sweaters out from the back of our closets and cozying up in front of the fire with a hot cup of tea and, of course, a cupcake!

Delicious Memories

SEPTEMBER 1986

We were little girls in the first and third grade and living in Hamilton, Ontario. Our grandparents, Paschalis (Ben) and Katherine Ouzas (we called them Babee and Papou), lived down the street from us in their cozy 1950s bungalow. Our parents, Ilias and Elaine Kallinis, both worked. Our father was a property manager and our mother worked at a bank, so we would stay with our grandparents till they arrived home around seven o'clock. Every day, we walked the twelve blocks from Sir Isaac Brock Elementary School together to our grandparents' place, where Babee was anxiously waiting for us. If the weather was icy or snowy, she would sit in a chair right in front of the door, finally breathing a sigh of relief when we burst through it. We think we inherited our talent for worrying from her; we constantly worry about everything!

We had a little ritual for when we arrived. Before we did our homework in the living room, before we turned on Oprah on the TV, we'd go into the kitchen. Babee would always have a sweet treat waiting for us: a fresh pastry horn, a cupcake, or a biscotti cookie.

> *Their relationship was an inspiration to us of what a strong, loving marriage should be.*

She cooked and baked all day long; baking was something that was passed down from generation to generation in our family. Growing up in Proti, a small village in Greece, Babee had learned by watching her mother and grandmother. They didn't have fancy appliances, only wood stoves and ovens, and all the ingredients were fresh from their land—their cows, their chickens, their gardens.

We sat around the small kitchen table; our grandparents had a cup of coffee and we each had a cup of warm milk. Babee would put a pinch of instant coffee in our milk, so we felt like grown-ups drinking "coffee," too! We talked about our day at school—how we did on our math or spelling test—and Babee and Papou listened patiently and nodded their approval. They loved it when we did well in our classes. They were both so proud of us, and we were proud of them. They were extremely close, and we can never remember them arguing. Their relationship was an inspiration to us of what a strong, loving marriage should be. We cherished hearing the story of how they fell in love before World War II: Papou left to go fight in the Greek army and told Babee that he would come back to marry her. He did.

After the war, many people in our grandparents' village moved to the United States, Australia, and Canada to start a new and better life. In the early 1950s, our grandfather traveled to Boston and Toronto to try to find a job. He traveled along the East Coast and finally found a position as a construction foreman outside Toronto, in a small town called Hamilton. He bought a house and slowly, he brought the members of his family over. Mommy was seven years old when she came to Canada.

Clockwise from top right: Babee in her kitchen; Papou in Greece as a young man; Babee and Papou on their sixtieth wedding anniversary, November 1994

When our grandfather passed away in March 1996, Babee was heartbroken. We had never seen her so sad; it was like a piece of her was gone forever. It was a very difficult time and she missed him dearly. She died exactly one hundred days after Papou.

But the years they had together, and the years they shared with us, were filled with affection and devotion. Babee showed her love for her family by baking. She had two kitchens in her house—one downstairs and one upstairs. The baking was always done in the upstairs "special" kitchen. We remember her lime-green 1950s refrigerator and stove, her lace curtains, and her dark oak cabinets. There was a Marks & Spencer cookie jar on the counter—always full of cookies she had baked—and we'd stand on tiptoe, trying to reach it!

On the stove was her old-fashioned silver tea kettle, and hanging on the oven handle were her flower-printed oven mitts. Her cabinets were brimming with canisters of flour and sugar and cinnamon and a million other fragrant spices. The kitchen always had a sweet sugary scent to it, like something had just come out of the oven. It felt warm and safe, and just being in this environment instantly erased any chill from the outside. If we had had a bad day at school, or if we had argued on the walk home, everything would be completely forgotten as soon as we entered Babee's kitchen.

We did this every day for fourteen years. While some kids would break out potato chips, pretzels, or cheese and crackers after school, we would always have Babee's sweet homemade treats—and love—to savor.

Caramel Apple Cupcakes

Our grandparents had an apple tree in their backyard, so most of the apples Babee used in her baking were fresh picked. We loved picking the apples! The tree was tall, so we would have to get on the stepladder to reach the ripest ones and then put them in buckets. It would be chilly, so we would bundle up in our sweaters and take turns on the ladder with our grandfather directing us. Sometimes, if we weren't careful, the apples would fall off and bop us on the head. After we'd pick them, we'd help our grandmother peel the apples, and then place them in a bowl of water with a little lemon so they wouldn't brown. Babee never used an apple corer. She was so skilled with her little paring knife that we could never peel as fast as she could!

We still love baking with apples today. There's something about the smell of apples and cinnamon in the oven that's just heavenly. This cupcake has been on our September menu ever since we opened. To us, this flavor captures the feeling of September and the apple tree in our grandparents' backyard. The caramel reminds us of the caramel pudding our grandmother used to make (see recipe, page 24), and gives it an extra-special touch.

Makes 18 cupcakes

FOR THE CUPCAKES

2 ½ cups all-purpose flour

3 teaspoons baking powder

1 teaspoon ground cinnamon

½ teaspoon salt

16 tablespoons unsalted butter, at room temperature (European style recommended)

2 cups sugar

4 large eggs, at room temperature

⅓ cup hot water

2 ½ cups freshly grated apples (4 to 5 medium-size apples—we use Gala apples, but you can use your favorite type)

FOR THE VANILLA CREAM-CHEESE FROSTING

4 tablespoons unsalted butter, at room
temperature (European style
recommended)

4 cups confectioners' sugar, sifted

¼ teaspoon pure vanilla extract
(Nielsen-Massey pure Madagascar
Bourbon recommended)

6 ounces cream cheese, at room temperature

FOR THE CARAMEL   *Makes 2 ½ cups caramel*

2 cups sugar

1 tablespoon water

12 tablespoons unsalted butter, at room
temperature (European style
recommended)

1 teaspoon pure vanilla extract (Nielsen-
Massey pure Madagascar Bourbon
recommended)

1 cup heavy cream, at room temperature

For the cupcakes:

❶ Preheat the oven to 350°F. Line a standard cupcake pan with twelve paper baking cups, and a second pan with six baking cups, or grease pans with butter if not using baking cups.

❷ Sift together the flour, baking powder, cinnamon, and salt on a sheet of parchment paper or wax paper and set aside.

❸ Place the butter in the bowl of a stand mixer or in a bowl with a handheld electric mixer. Beat on medium speed until fluffy. Stop to add the sugar; beat on medium speed until well incorporated, approximately 3 to 5 minutes.

4 Add the eggs one at a time, mixing slowly on medium speed, after each addition. It's important to add them one at a time so that they will completely incorporate into the batter and you don't put too much weight on your batter at once. This would collapse all the little air bubbles you created when you creamed the butter and sugar.

5 Reduce the speed to low. At this stage, it's always important to mix as slowly and as little as necessary since you don't want to traumatize your batter. Add one third of the flour mixture to the butter mixture, then gradually add one third of the hot water, beating until well incorporated. Add another third of the flour mixture, followed by one third of the hot water. It's important to add the flour and water little by little like this, so that your batter does not have too much weight thrown on it and that you allow each amount of flour and water to completely mix into the batter. Stop to scrape down the bowl as needed. Add the remaining flour mixture, followed by the remaining hot water, and beat just until combined.

6 Using a spatula, fold the grated apple into the batter. Take care not to overmix the batter. If you overmix the batter, the cupcakes will not be light and fluffy but instead very dense.

7 Use a standard-size ice-cream scoop to fill each baking cup with batter, so the cups are two-thirds full. Bake for 18 to 20 minutes (start checking at 15 minutes) or until a toothpick inserted into the center of a cupcake comes out clean. After 5 minutes, transfer the cupcakes to a wire rack to cool completely for approximately 20 minutes.

how to stuff a cupcake

Sometimes it's nice to have a little surprise in the center when you bite into a cupcake. This recipe has caramel that oozes out (yum!). To get that caramel right in the center, line up cooled cupcakes on a sheet of wax paper so you don't get caramel on your counter. Using an apple corer, gently remove the center of each cupcake, cutting all the way through the cupcake till you hit the paper baking cup, then pour the cooled caramel into a plastic squeeze bottle or a pastry bag and squeeze caramel filling into the center of each cupcake. Make sure your cupcakes are cooled or they could collapse if you try to core them when they are too hot. You can use this technique to fill your cupcakes with frosting, chocolate ganache, preserves, fudge, marshmallow, and anything else your heart desires! ✱

It's always best to cool the cupcakes at room temperature. Putting them in the refrigerator to cool can dry out the cake.

For the vanilla cream-cheese frosting:

Place all ingredients in the bowl of an electric mixer fitted with the paddle attachment; beat until well combined. Be sure to beat on high speed at the very end for at least 2 minutes to ensure that the frosting is light and fluffy.

For the caramel:

Pour the sugar and water into a large saucepan. Heat on medium-high heat and stir constantly until the sugar completely liquefies. Stir constantly and be careful not to burn the sugar. After all the sugar has dissolved, add the butter and vanilla extract to the saucepan and mix thoroughly. Once the butter has melted and the butter and sugar are completely mixed, remove from heat and, using a whisk, slowly whisk in the heavy cream until you reach a beautiful golden brown caramel color. Set aside and let cool and thicken for 5 minutes at room temperature. Refrigerate for 20 minutes to thicken further before you use to fill or decorate.

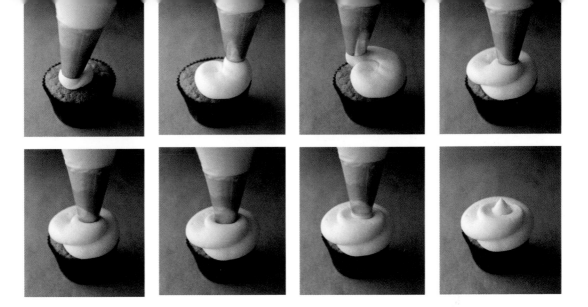

The Georgetown Cupcake Signature Swirl

The frosting on our cupcakes has a certain "style" to it—a perfect little cloud that reaches a pretty peak in the center. It's just the perfect amount of frosting—not too much, not too little—and it looks neat and sweet! Everyone is always asking us how to do it. So here, without further ado, is our secret!

For this recipe, transfer the vanilla cream-cheese frosting into a plastic disposable piping bag, fitted with a large round metal tip. Be sure to whip up your frosting so it is light and airy. You don't need to twist the top of your bag—you can just hold it closed with one hand and use your other hand to hold the bag near the bottom and squeeze.

Start in the center of the cupcake, applying pressure to the bottom of the bag, and guide the tip around the cupcake in a circular motion, then end in the center with a burst of pressure. Try to move quickly and confidently. If you go too slowly, the frosting may come out uneven. You can then add your decorations. For this cupcake, take the squeeze bottle of caramel and drizzle a flower pattern (or pattern of your choice) on top of each cupcake. You could also top with an apple slice, a sprinkling of cinnamon, or a piece of hand-shaped apple fondant!

Babee's Caramel Pudding

We *loved* Babee's caramel pudding when we were little girls. In her upstairs fridge, there would often be eight little round glass dishes of it, all lined up, waiting for us. The dishes were equally special: they were vintage and had white flowers etched on the side and tiny matching spoons. We remember being so impatient during dinner, anticipating the pudding for dessert. We would run like the wind upstairs and get our pudding as soon as the dinner dishes were cleared. We used to dance around the kitchen, scraping our pudding dishes while we ate it!

Makes 8 servings of 6 ounces each

2 ½ cups whole milk, plus an additional ½ cup to dissolve the cornstarch

1 cup heavy cream

6 tablespoons cornstarch

4 eggs, at room temperature

1 teaspoon pure vanilla extract (Nielsen-Massey vanilla extract recommended)

seeds from 2 vanilla beans

1 cup sugar

1 teaspoon salt

4 tablespoons unsalted butter, cubed, at room temperature (European style recommended)

2 cups caramel, plus ½ cup for drizzling on top of each pudding dish (see recipe, page 20)

❶ In a large saucepan over medium-high heat, bring 2 ½ cups milk and the heavy cream to a gentle boil. Be careful not to scald the milk.

❷ In the bowl of a stand mixer or in a bowl with a handheld electric mixer, mix the cornstarch in ½ cup whole milk. Add the eggs one at a time, followed by the vanilla extract, the vanilla bean seeds, the sugar, and the salt, mixing on low speed after each addition.

❸ While mixing on low speed, add the hot milk and cream very slowly.

4 Pour the mixture back into the large saucepan and, using a whisk, stir constantly over medium-high heat. Add the cubed butter, stirring constantly, and watch as the mixture slowly thickens and reaches a pudding consistency. This process should take approximately 5 to 10 minutes.

5 After the mixture thickens, slowly add 2 cups caramel and whisk vigorously. Be sure to continuously whisk the mixture or else lumps will form (or whisk to remove all lumps). Cook for an additional 2 to 3 minutes and remove from heat. Let pudding cool for 5 minutes in the pot, then pour into serving dishes. Let the pudding come to room temperature, then refrigerate the pudding in serving dishes for at least 1 hour. This pudding tastes even better the next day, after it's been chilled overnight. Before serving, using a squeeze bottle, squeeze the remaining ½ cup caramel in a flower pattern on top of the pudding in each dish.

Tricks and Treats

HALLOWEEN 1987

When we were kids, October meant one thing to us: Halloween. Actually, that's probably still true for us today! The whole month is built on the anticipation of a massive sugar overload. We couldn't wait to go trick-or-treating and would count down the days until the thirty-first. We'd spend the whole month deciding on our costumes. Every year they'd be different: we dressed up as artists, chefs, princesses, firefighters, Cinderella, Mother Nature, cats—everything under the sun! But our favorite costumes were the Greek dancer outfits we wore when we were nine and ten. Mommy dressed us in long skirts with sequined edges, sequin aprons, and colorful sequin head scarves with jingling faux-gold coins stitched to the edges. We were the envy of all our friends—nobody else had costumes like ours!

We went trick-or-treating in our neighborhood and made our way down the street to our grandparents' house. Babee had an extra-special Halloween bag ready for us with Greek shortbread cookies called Melomakarona, a citrusy walnut cookie. She also had a full-size Kit Kat bar in there—we *loved* Kit Kats—and a five-dollar bill. We were so excited! We went home at the end of the evening and dumped out our bags on the floor and organized all our candy. We traded and, of course, fought over who got more of what, but in the end we just shared.

Babee, Mommy, Sophie, and Katherine, Halloween 1981

Even more important than our costumes and candy, though, was the tradition of baking Halloween treats. Most kids just love Halloween for the chocolate bars, gummies, and lollipops. For us, though, Halloween meant that we could bake up a storm of scary sweets. We couldn't wait for our school Halloween parties. We would make everything from ghost cookies to bat brownies, and of course, all kinds of spooky-themed cupcakes!

Our cupcakes were the most popular at our elementary-school parties. Babee would help us bake them in silver foil baking cups. Everyone skipped over the sugar cookies and Rice Krispies treats and made a beeline for them. We always baked rich chocolate cupcakes for Halloween, never vanilla. To us, chocolate was a scarier flavor—something about the color of rich fudge conjured up images of midnight and graveyards! We would top them with bright orange buttercream frosting, spread on thick with a spatula (this was *way* before we developed our signature swirl), and then sprinkle black, purple, and green candy jimmies on top or cover them with mini

M&Ms, candy-bar pieces, or a peanut-butter-cup wedge. We took great pride in the fact that our friends and classmates loved so much something that we baked. We brought the plastic container home empty—not even a crumb left behind.

As we got a little more adept at baking, our Halloween cupcake art improved as well. We'd drizzle fudge on top of the frosting in concentric circles and then drag a toothpick through the fudge circles to connect them and make a spiderweb pattern. We'd then put jelly spiders on top of the fudge webs. We'd also carve white marshmallows into ghosts and twist black licorice into sculpted black cats.

Halloween is the time to break out all the candy and bright food color and let yourself capture the spirit (pun intended!) of this spooky holiday. Your cupcakes don't have to be refined or elegant. Halloween cupcakes are about thrills, chills, and things that creep you out!

> *Halloween cupcakes are about thrills, chills, and things that creep you out!*

Chocolate Goo-nache Cupcakes

This cupcake is based on our Chocolate Ganache cupcake—which was crowned best cupcake in *The Washington Post*'s Cupcake Wars!

Makes 18 cupcakes

FOR THE CUPCAKES
1 ¼ cups all-purpose flour
½ teaspoon baking soda
¼ teaspoon salt
8 tablespoons European-style unsalted butter, at room temperature (Plugrá recommended)
1 ¼ cups sugar

2 large eggs, at room temperature
1 ¼ teaspoons pure vanilla extract (preferably Madagascar Bourbon)
1 cup whole milk, at room temperature
½ cup Valrhona cocoa powder, sifted (may substitute another good-quality cocoa powder)

FOR THE MARSHMALLOW "GOO"

8 cups small marshmallows

4 tablespoons butter, at room temperature

½ teaspoon pure vanilla extract

1 drop gel green food color

FOR THE GANACHE FROSTING

½ cup heavy cream

1 cup Callebaut semisweet chocolate
chips (may substitute other good-quality
semisweet chocolate chips)

FOR THE DECORATION

4 cups of crushed Oreo cookies

vanilla buttercream frosting (see recipe, page 133)

white fondant

green food color

black food color

For the cupcakes:

1 Preheat the oven to 350°F. Line a standard cupcake pan with twelve paper baking cups, and a second pan with six baking cups, or grease pans with butter if not using baking cups.

2 Sift together the flour, baking soda, and salt on a sheet of parchment paper or wax paper and set aside.

3 Place the butter in the bowl of a stand mixer or in a bowl with a handheld electric mixer. Beat on medium speed until fluffy. Stop to add the sugar; then beat on medium speed until well incorporated. Add the eggs one at a time, mixing slowly after each addition.

4 Combine the vanilla extract and milk in a large liquid measuring cup.

5 Reduce the speed to low. Add one third of the flour mixture to the butter mixture, then gradually add one third of the milk mixture, beating until well incorporated. Add another third of the flour mixture, followed by one third of the milk mixture. Stop to scrape down the bowl as needed. Add the remaining flour mixture, followed by the remaining milk mixture, and mix slowly until just combined.

6 Add the cocoa powder, mixing on low speed until just incorporated.

7 Use a standard-size ice-cream scoop to fill each baking cup with batter, so that the wells are two-thirds full. Bake for 18 to 20 minutes (start checking at 15 minutes) or until a toothpick inserted into the center of a cupcake comes out clean. Transfer the pan to a wire rack to cool completely.

8 After the cupcakes have cooled, poke each cupcake with an apple corer and push it all the way through. Be careful not to rip through the baking cup. Remove the cupcake core. (We like to save the cores and eat them later!)

For the marshmallow "goo":

1 Next, melt down the marshmallows, butter, and vanilla in a medium saucepan on medium heat. Keep an eye on the saucepan to make sure the marshmallows don't burn. Once the marshmallows are melted completely, add a drop of green food color to the saucepan. Mix thoroughly. Add more green food color until you get your desired color of green. Next, transfer the marshmallow "goo" to a squeeze bottle using a ladle or spoon.

> **sisters' baking secret**
> ## a "sticky" situation
> Working with marshmallow can be tricky! Try to work as quickly as possible before the marshmallow firms up. It's a good idea to keep your marshmallow pliable and warm in a warm pot until the very last second you need it. If it seizes up, you can reheat it. ✖

2 Squeeze your green marshmallow "goo" into each cupcake core until you reach the top.

For the ganache frosting:

1 Lay a large piece of wax paper on your counter or work surface.

❷ Combine the heavy cream and chocolate in a medium heatproof bowl. Fill a medium saucepan with an inch or two of water and place over medium-low heat. Place the bowl over the saucepan and let the mixture melt, stirring continuously until it is shiny and smooth.

❸ Remove the bowl of chocolate ganache from the saucepan; let it cool slightly for 2 to 3 minutes. Working with one cupcake at a time, carefully dip each cupcake top in the warm ganache, twisting your wrist as needed to make sure the cupcake top gets completely coated. To prevent drips, quickly turn the cupcake right side up and place on the wax paper. Allow the ganache to set for 5 minutes before proceeding.

For the decoration:

❶ Cover the tops of each of your cupcakes with crushed Oreo cookie crumbles to look like dirt. Then fit a plastic piping bag with a multiopening "grass" tip. Fill your icing bag with green-tinted vanilla buttercream frosting (see recipe, page 133). Pipe long strokes of grass on either side of the grave.

❷ Next, it is time to make the tombstone. Add a touch of black food color to white fondant to result in a silvery gray color. Make sure to knead the fondant using your hands or a rolling pin so the color is even. Once the color is consistent, roll out the fondant with a rolling pin on a sheet of waxed paper or parchment paper until you have a smooth, thin sheet of fondant. The sheet should be about ¼-inch thick, but this does not need to be exact. Using a knife or a scalpel, cut in the shape of a tombstone. You can cut as many tombstones as you want out of the same sheet of fondant. Next, remove the excess fondant so you are left with the tombstones on the wax paper. Using a scalpel, carve "RIP" into the fondant. Then, slide a knife or a pastry scraper underneath each tombstone so they don't stick to the wax paper. Wait till the fondant hardens, usually 20 to 25 minutes. Stick each tombstone in the grass area on top of each cupcake. For more on working with fondant, see page 60.

Recipe for Success

Inspiration Is All Around You

We love walking around outside in October and admiring all the beautiful old trees in Georgetown. As the leaves begin to change, they turn the most captivating colors: fiery reds, toasty auburns, and golden yellows. These beautiful October leaves were the inspiration for our Pumpkin Spice cupcakes. We decided to pair a pumpkin spice cake with a maple cream-cheese frosting (see recipe, page 36), and decorate it so when people looked at them, they could get a little taste of what we see. We top the cupcakes with beautiful golden brown, red, and orange fondant leaves and dust them with an edible bronze glitter, giving them a little extra sparkle.

If we're ever feeling stumped to come up with a new cupcake flavor, we simply remind ourselves that inspiration is everywhere. So many of our cupcakes come from things we see or experience. But this lesson doesn't apply just to baking. Sometimes in life, you're feeling stuck and need to jump-start your creative juices. Our advice: take a deep breath and keep your eyes and your mind wide open to every possibility. Something small—like a crimson leaf floating on the breeze—may just spark your imagination and it will take flight.

Pumpkin Spice Cupcakes

Every October as kids, we loved to go pumpkin picking and buy fresh pumpkins. We would always look for the perfectly short and round ones—we didn't like the tall skinny ones. It was difficult to pick out the perfect pumpkin, and we'd often argue about whether or not the pumpkin was the exact right shape.

When we got home from the pumpkin patch, our grandfather would help us carve our pumpkins. Papou was an amazing handyman—he worked in construction and built most of our grandparents' houses as well as furniture for us and for our dolls. Our jack-o'-lanterns were never really that complex: we opted for the more traditional look of just eyes, a nose, and jagged teeth. The best part of the process to us, though, was pulling out the "pumpkin guts." It was stinky and goopy and slippery, and it made a wonderful mess!

Our grandmother would take the pumpkin flesh and bake it in the oven with a little cinnamon and sugar, and then we'd stick it in the blender, puree it, and use it for baking. We'd bake pumpkin bread, pumpkin cake, and pumpkin pie, and we would also roast the pumpkin seeds in the oven. Really, she used every single part of that pumpkin! The thing we loved the most was our grandmother's pumpkin cake. It was more of a cake-bread hybrid: very dense and savory yet sweet. It smelled *amazing* coming out of the oven. We would sometimes just eat it without any icing, hot from the oven. We'd burn our tongues because we wouldn't even wait for it to cool!

Makes 24 cupcakes

FOR THE CUPCAKES

2 ½ cups all-purpose flour

3 teaspoons baking powder

2 teaspoons ground cinnamon

1 teaspoon allspice

1 teaspoon ground nutmeg

½ teaspoon salt

16 tablespoons unsalted butter, at room temperature

2 cups sugar

4 eggs

1 ½ cups pumpkin puree (homemade preferred, but you can also use canned puree)

2 tablespoons honey

⅓ cup hot water

FOR THE MAPLE CREAM-CHEESE FROSTING

8 tablespoons unsalted butter, at room
    temperature
8 cups confectioners' sugar, sifted
½ teaspoon pure vanilla extract
12 ounces cream cheese, at room temperature
½ cup pure maple syrup

FOR THE DECORATION

small package of white fondant (available at
    most craft or baking supply stores)
brown, red, and yellow food color
gold and brown edible luster dust (optional,
    available at most craft or baking supply stores)

For the cupcakes:

1 Preheat the oven to 350°F. Line two standard cupcake pans with twelve paper baking cups each, or grease pans with butter if not using baking cups.

2 Sift together the flour, baking powder, cinnamon, allspice, nutmeg, and salt on a sheet of parchment paper or wax paper and set aside.

3 Place the butter in the bowl of a stand mixer or in a bowl with a handheld electric mixer. Beat on medium speed until fluffy. Stop to add the sugar; then beat on medium speed until well incorporated.

4 Add the eggs one at a time, mixing slowly after each addition. Mix in the pumpkin puree and honey. Reduce the speed to low. Add one third of the flour mixture to the butter mixture, then gradually add one third of the hot water, beating until well incorporated. Add another third of the flour mixture, followed by one third of the hot water. Stop to scrape down the bowl as needed. Add the remaining flour mixture, followed by the remaining hot water, and mix slowly until just combined. Take care not to overmix the batter so the cupcakes will bake up light and fluffy.

5 Use a standard-size ice-cream scoop to fill each baking cup with batter, so the wells are two-thirds full. Bake for 25 to 30 minutes (start checking at 20 minutes) or until a toothpick inserted into the center of a cupcake comes out clean. Transfer the pan to a wire rack to cool completely.

For the frosting:

Place all ingredients in the bowl of an electric mixer fitted with the paddle attachment; beat until well combined. Be sure to beat on high speed for at least two minutes at the end to ensure that the frosting is light and fluffy.

For the decoration:

1 Line up cooled cupcakes on a sheet of wax paper. Transfer the maple cream-cheese frosting into a plastic piping bag fitted with a large round metal tip (or piping tip of your choice). Apply a signature swirl (see page 23).

2 Break white fondant into three equal pieces. Add a small drop of red food color to one piece of fondant, a small drop of yellow food color to the second piece of fondant, and a small drop of brown food color to the third piece of fondant. Using your hands, knead the color into each piece of fondant so the color is uniform throughout. If you'd like the colors to be darker or more intense, add more food color and repeat. Then, starting with one piece of fondant, use a rolling pin to roll the fondant out to a thin sheet. Dust with edible luster dust (optional). Using a mini leaf cookie cutter, cut out leaf shapes and place on top of each cupcake. For more on working with fondant, see page 60.

Love and Maple Syrup

NOVEMBER 1980

When we were little girls, we lived for those lazy Saturday mornings when we would wake up, run downstairs in our pj's, and turn on the TV to watch cartoons. While we sat mesmerized by *She-Ra: Princess of Power* and *Doctor Snuggles,* Mommy would be in the kitchen, whipping up her famous pancakes.

We never ate pancakes during the week—Monday through Friday, we ate cereal, toast, or eggs. It was only on Saturdays that Mommy made her specialty. Babee made pancakes as well, but hers were either a thicker Greek version called *tiganites,* or the French-style thin crepes, topped with powdered sugar and fresh strawberries. Mommy had her own formula for traditional pancakes that made our mouths water. She never had a recipe; it was all from memory. She knew exactly how much flour and milk and sugar to add to the bowl to give the batter the right consistency. Once she dropped the batter onto the frying pan, the smell would waft through the house, summoning us to the kitchen to watch Mommy in action. If we were *really* lucky, she would add chocolate chips, blueberries, or strawberries. She'd flip them high in the air, creating stacks upon stacks of golden cakes. We'd gobble them up, pouring on tons of maple syrup till they were swimming in it.

For Mommy, pancakes are all about love. You see, our parents first met over a pancake breakfast. It was 1968, and Mommy was a teenager working at a restaurant at the bus station in Hamilton, Canada. One day during her shift, the short-order chef offered to make her a pancake breakfast. Mommy was embarrassed by the gesture—and she wasn't particularly hungry—but she couldn't be rude and say no. The chef brought out the biggest pancake Mommy had ever seen! She didn't just want to take a bite or two and leave the rest to waste and insult the chef, but there was no way she could eat the enormous sweet concoction that was put in front of her. She stared at the plate and had no idea how she could get out of this situation gracefully.

Mommy and Daddy, 2005

Then she looked up at the chef: Gee, he was cute! And much to her relief, he had a solution. He asked if he could share the giant pancake with her. So there they sat at the counter, talking and laughing, and eating the giant pancake off the same plate. Little did they know this was the first of many pancakes they would share. The courtship was on! But to her credit,

Mommy was no pushover and made our father wait a few years before they married in 1970.

We loved this story—and Mommy still loves to tell it. Even as we got older, we continued this tradition of lazy Saturday breakfast—and, of course, we had to create a maple cupcake to help us relive our childhood and the story of our parents falling in love over pancakes.

sisters' baking secret
flipping the perfect pancake

Mommy is the master of this trick!

• Make sure the pan is fully heated up to medium-high.

• Add a small amount of butter to the pan just before you put the batter in. You don't need too much, just enough to coat the bottom of the pan.

• Don't try to cook too many pancakes at once, and don't make them too big! Pancake batter will expand in the pan—make sure there is plenty of room between the pancakes so you can maneuver the spatula and flip the pancakes without knocking the other ones in the pan.

• Finally, you need to use the Goldilocks approach to timing. If you flip too soon, the pancake will break apart. If you flip too late, the bottom will be burned. Keep an eye on the pancakes, and once they start to bubble a little on top, it is time to flip, and with any luck, they will be the perfect golden brown! ✱

Maple Chocolate Chip Cupcakes

Makes 12 cupcakes

2 ½ cups all-purpose flour

½ teaspoon baking powder

¼ teaspoon salt

8 tablespoons unsalted butter, at room
   temperature

1 ¾ cups sugar

2 large eggs, at room temperature

2 ¼ teaspoons pure vanilla extract

seeds from 1 vanilla bean

1 ¼ cups whole milk, at room temperature

½ cup pure maple syrup

½ cup chocolate chips

For the cupcakes:

1 Preheat the oven to 350°F. Line a cupcake pan with twelve paper baking cups, or grease the pan with butter if not using baking cups.

2 Sift together the flour, baking powder, and salt on a piece of parchment paper or wax paper and set aside.

3 Place the unsalted butter in the bowl of a stand mixer or in a bowl with a handheld electric mixer. Add the sugar; beat on medium speed until well incorporated.

4 Add the eggs one at a time, mixing slowly after each addition.

5 Combine the vanilla extract, vanilla bean seeds, and milk in a large liquid measuring cup.

6 Reduce the speed to low. Add one third of the flour mixture to the butter mixture, then gradually add one third of the milk mixture, beating until well incorporated. Add another third of the flour mixture, followed by one third of the milk mixture.

Stop to scrape down the bowl as needed. Add the remaining flour mixture, followed by the remaining milk mixture, and mix slowly until just combined.

7 Add in the maple syrup and mix slowly until just combined.

8 Gently fold in the chocolate chips, just until incorporated.

9 Scoop batter into baking cups so that they are two-thirds full and bake for 18 to 20 minutes (start checking at 15 minutes) or until a toothpick inserted into the center of a cupcake comes out clean. Transfer the pan to a wire rack to cool completely.

Whipped Chocolate Ganache Frosting

This variation on our chocolate ganache frosting still has only two ingredients, but it's a little trickier to make since you need to chill it to achieve the right consistency to frost the cupcakes versus dipping them in the ganache. However, the end result is a beautiful Maple Chocolate Chip cupcake with a beautiful signature swirl (see page 23) of chocolate ganache frosting.

2 cups good-quality semisweet chocolate chips (Callebaut brand recommended)

1 cup heavy cream

(see page 23)

---

sisters' baking secret
melting chocolate

We always like to melt chocolate over a double boiler or in a glass bowl placed over a pot of boiling water. This ensures that the chocolate will melt slowly and will be less likely to burn. To melt chocolate, fill a saucepan half-full with water and bring the water to a gentle rolling boil. Place the chocolate in a heatproof bowl, such as a glass bowl, and place the bowl over the pot. Now stir, stir, stir. If you leave the chocolate too long, it can scorch. Chocolate left unattended for a long time can overheat and get grainy. Once the water reaches a boil, turn the heat to low so the chocolate is melting over low heat. You can put the chocolate in the bowl before the water comes to a boil. We like to use chocolate chips or chunks, but if you are melting down a bar of chocolate, be sure to chop it into uniform pieces so it will melt evenly. It doesn't take a very long time: you can usually melt 1 cup of chocolate in 10 minutes or less. Milk chocolate melts more quickly than dark chocolate (which doesn't contain milk)—so keep that in mind! ✪

For the Frosting:

Fill a medium saucepan with 1 to 2 inches water and place over medium-low heat. Place the chocolate chips and heavy cream in a medium glass bowl over the saucepan and melt the chocolate chips. Stir occasionally until the chips are completely melted. Remove the bowl of melted chocolate from the saucepan and let it come to room temperature. Then cover the bowl with plastic wrap and place it in the refrigerator for one hour or until it reaches the consistency of peanut butter. Using a spatula, whip up the ganache and place it in a plastic piping bag fitted with a large round metal tip. Frost each Maple Chocolate Chip cupcake with Georgetown Cupcake's signature swirl (see page 23) of whipped chocolate ganache frosting.

THANKSGIVING 2008

We'll never forget our first Thanksgiving at Georgetown Cupcake. The day before, we thought, *We won't be that busy. Most people buy pies for Thanksgiving.* We had a very small staff scheduled because many of our student employees had gone home for their school break. So we opened our doors with a skeleton crew expecting a nice, quiet day. We were so wrong! Instead, we had a line of customers who were ordering one, two, or three dozen cupcakes each! Everyone was on their way home for Thanksgiving and wanted to bring Georgetown Cupcakes to their families. Our front counter staff was packing boxes like mad, and the two of us were packing preorders furiously, snatching the cupcakes off of the racks as soon as they came out.

We loved the idea that our cupcakes were now part of people's family holidays.

After the day was over and we closed the door, we were mentally and physically drained. There was not one cupcake left and the shop looked like a tornado had blown through. We had just survived our first Thanksgiving at the shop. We had both worked so hard, but in a way, it was exhilarating for us. We loved the idea that our cupcakes were now part of people's family holidays.

The next day was Thanksgiving—one of the rare days we close the shop—and as we all gathered together over a turkey dinner, we were especially grateful. Not just for our business that was booming, but also for all the people in our circle, not just around the table, but those in our hearts, minds, and memories.

When we were younger, Babee would create Thanksgiving feasts that would keep us full for days. Of course, the centerpiece of every Thanksgiving dinner is a beautiful turkey, with savory, smooth gravy and succulent stuffing. We would also stuff ourselves with baked potatoes, rice with spinach and mushrooms, and fresh, homemade bread.

Babee incorporated some of her favorite Greek recipes into our Thanksgiving dinner. We would start the feast with piping-hot Avgolemono soup, a delicious chicken noodle soup with a tempered egg and a hint of lemon. She would make a giant Greek salad, as pleasing to the eyes as it was to the stomach, filled with lettuce, tomato, cucumbers, black olives, feta cheese, oregano, olive oil, and vinegar. And we would have a cheese platter and all kinds of different peppers that were fried, stuffed, and pickled.

Papou took great pride in Thanksgiving as well. He would buy grapes by the bushel and make his own Greek wine. We were too young to drink it, but he assured us that he had the best wine in all of Canada. Babee, not to be bested, incorporated her fantastic baking into every course. For dinner, she would also create paper-thin phyllo dough stuffed with cheese and spinach or with pumpkin. For dessert, she also baked a traditional Greek cake called Revani, piercing holes in the top with a fork and pouring in syrup to make it sinfully sweet.

Babee's Revani Cake

Makes one 9-inch round cake

1 ¼ cups all-purpose flour

1 cup semolina

2 ½ teaspoons baking powder

¼ teaspoon salt

8 tablespoons unsalted butter, at room temperature (European style recommended)

1 ¼ cups sugar

3 large eggs, at room temperature

1 teaspoon pure vanilla extract

seeds from 1 vanilla bean

2 large lemons, zested

1 ¼ cup whole milk, at room temperature

CITRUS SYRUP

1 ¾ cups sugar

1 ½ cups water

1 orange, zested

1 large lemon, zested

2 teaspoons fresh-squeezed lemon juice

Recipe for Success

Babee Always Told Us, "Family Comes First."

We try to remember this, especially when we get stressed out at the bakery. Things may be hectic, flour may be flying, but we have each other's back: family first, business second. In life, it's easy to put family time on the back burner and your career or business aspirations first. You get swept away in the everyday minutiae. But in the end, if you don't have people around you to share your success with, or to love you and support you, you are like a cupcake without the frosting. We do not take our family (especially each other) and their love for granted, and it has helped us so much in our journey both starting and running our bakery.

Our last family vacation before starting Georgetown Cupcake, Thanksgiving 2007

For the cake:

1 Preheat the oven to 350°F and grease a 9-inch round cake pan with unsalted butter.

2 Sift together the flour, semolina, baking powder, and salt on a piece of parchment paper or wax paper and set aside.

3 In the bowl of a stand mixer or in a bowl with a handheld electric mixer, cream together the butter and sugar until light and fluffy. Add the eggs one at a time, mixing slowly after each addition.

4 Add vanilla extract, vanilla bean seeds, and lemon zest and mix.

5 Add one third of the flour mixture, then one third of the milk, followed by one third of the flour mixture, one third of the milk, and then the last third of the flour mixture and the last third of the milk, mixing after each addition. Scrape down the bowl with a spatula as needed.

6 Pour the batter into the pan and bake 40 to 45 minutes or until a toothpick comes out clean.

For the syrup:

1 Bring the sugar, water, orange zest, lemon zest, and lemon juice to a boil in a small pot. Reduce heat to medium and simmer for 6 to 7 minutes.

2 Pierce holes into the top of the cake using a fork and pour slightly cooled syrup over the cake, so that it is absorbed into the cake.

Part 2

··

WINTER

*Winter is the most magical season,
especially in DC. Snowflakes dancing in
the air, the crunch of snow under your
feet, kids making snow angels in the park,
icicles lining tree branches. Just close your
eyes and you can see it—and smell it!
The fragrant aroma of cinnamon and
nutmeg filling the entire house.
There's a lot of baking to do!*

4. ◉ DECEMBER

A Taste of Home

In our family, we would have one relative, usually Nicholas, our youngest male cousin, tasked to travel to everyone's home at Christmastime and pick up and drop off gifts from other relatives in our town. In addition to our grandparents, many of our aunts, uncles, and cousins lived in the same town as us. So along with the gifts, we would always send a basket of homemade baked goods with fruits and nuts. It was our family tradition, and it was taken very seriously. We'd pick out the best breads and cookies and cakes to wrap up and send to our relatives.

Christmas 1995 was not much different from previous years, but we will always cherish it. We did not know it at the time, but it was the last year we would share Christmas with Papou and Babee. Every year since, we feel their spirit when we gather around for Christmas dinner. We strive to live the lessons they taught us each Christmas and throughout the year. We are so grateful that they shared with us their infectious kindness, passion, and joy.

Sophie *(left),* Papou, and Katherine, Christmas 1982

Like all the years prior, Babee was in charge. Every family would get the same basketful of Greek breads, cakes, and Christmas cookies, and that meant a lot of baking. The oven was going all day, and as her helpers, we mentally prepared ourselves for the tall order. Babee did the heavy baking, and we were on decorating duty. As we grew older, we took on more roles in the kitchen: kneading and rolling the dough, brushing loaves with egg wash and sprinkling them with sesame seeds before they went into the oven. While the dough was rising, we would work on the cookies and cakes. There was never downtime the week of Christmas, but we enjoyed the challenge of it.

We made a lot of different traditional types of cookies: gingerbread, chocolate and vanilla sugar twists, and even rum shortbread cookies with walnuts in the middle. But it was the cakes that were the most fun. We made spice cake, gingerbread cake, a chocolate eggnog cake, and even chocolate peppermint cakes with crushed candy canes on top. Our favorite of all was the gingerbread cake. It had a goopy batter because of all the molasses, a lot different from our

> *Along with the gifts, we would always send a basket of homemade baked goods.*

other batters, but the cake always turned out amazing. We can still smell the nutmeg and cloves and picture the ooey, gooey molasses going into the batter.

Gingerbread Cupcakes with Cinnamon Cream-Cheese Frosting

Makes 12 cupcakes

FOR THE CUPCAKES

2 ¾ cups all-purpose flour

3 tablespoons ground ginger

2 teaspoons baking soda

1 ½ teaspoons ground cinnamon

½ teaspoon ground cloves

½ teaspoon ground nutmeg

¼ teaspoon salt

10 tablespoons unsalted butter, at room
    temperature

1 cup packed dark brown sugar

3 large eggs, at room temperature

1 ¼ cups molasses

1 cup hot water

FOR THE CINNAMON CREAM-CHEESE FROSTING

4 tablespoons unsalted butter, at room
    temperature

4 cups confectioners' sugar, sifted

¼ teaspoon pure vanilla extract

6 ounces cream cheese, at room temperature

2 teaspoons ground cinnamon

For the cupcakes:

❶ Preheat the oven to 350°F. Line a standard cupcake pan with twelve paper baking cups, or grease the pan with butter if not using baking cups.

❷ Sift together the dry ingredients, except for the brown sugar, and set aside. (We like to sift on a piece of parchment paper or wax paper so we can easily pick it up and pour it into our mixer, little by little.)

3 Cream together butter and brown sugar in the bowl of a stand mixer or in a bowl with a handheld electric mixer on high speed, 3 to 5 minutes, or until light and fluffy. Add the eggs one at a time, beating slowly after each addition. Add the molasses, mixing until well incorporated.

4 Add one third of the dry ingredients and one third of the water and mix thoroughly. Repeat. Stop to scrape down the bowl as needed. Add the last third of the dry ingredients and one third of the water, and mix thoroughly.

5 Scoop the batter into the cupcake pan using a standard-size ice-cream scoop.

6 Bake at 350°F for 16 to 18 minutes (start checking at 15 minutes) or until a toothpick comes out clean. Transfer the pan to a wire rack to cool completely.

For the frosting:

Place all ingredients in the bowl of an electric mixer fitted with the paddle attachment; beat until well combined. Frost cupcakes using Georgetown Cupcake's signature swirl (see page 23). We decorate our Gingerbread cupcakes with fondant gingerbread men with red candy buttons. You can use a mini gingerbread man cookie cutter and cut out fondant gingerbread men to place on top of your cupcakes to give them an extra-special festive touch!

(see page 23).

sisters' baking secret
perfect cupcakes every time

When Babee baked her spice cakes, she would give us the leftover batter and we would pour it into two tiny cake pans. We were probably toddlers the first time she allowed us to do this, and we remember sliding around the kitchen floor in our wool stockings and perching ourselves in front of the oven, cross-legged, watching our tiny cakes rise. We would see the air bubbles pop in the batter, and the cake slowly puff up. After about twenty minutes, Babee would open the oven and give us a toothpick to stick in the middle of our cakes, ever so gently, to make sure they were baked all the way through. These were probably the first cupcakes we ever made. To this day, we still use the toothpick test. We gently insert a toothpick and make sure there is no raw batter stuck to it. It is the best way to tell if your cupcakes are baked, but not overbaked. In general, we bake most of our cupcakes for 16 to 18 minutes, but we start checking at 15 minutes because the worst thing you can do is overbake your cupcakes and have them come out dry! ✱

Christmas at Georgetown Cupcake

The first day in December 2010, we started up the Christmas music—"Joy to the World," "It's Beginning to Look a Lot Like Christmas," "White Christmas"—all the classics. And, to the male employees' disappointment, the Mariah Carey Christmas hits! It's the

perfect soundtrack for whipping up Gingerbread cupcakes, Chocolate Peppermint cupcakes, White Chocolate Peppermint cupcakes, Chocolate Eggnog cupcakes, and more. The atmosphere in the shop immediately shifted into Christmas mode. Everyone wore a festive cardigan over their uniform. We even got pink Santa's hats for everyone to wear! We decorated the shop with silver garland and lights in the windows. Mommy went a little overboard with a life-size penguin she put in the corner of the shop and a lawn reindeer that she put on the coffee counter—but we let her keep them because they were just so cute!

We loved punching out little fondant reindeer and crushing up candy canes to sprinkle on the frosting. We decorated our vanilla cupcakes with shimmery pale-blue fondant snowflakes. There were even real snowflakes falling gently outside in Georgetown. It's our favorite month at the bakery—and also one of the busiest. So many people give cupcakes as gifts! Who wouldn't love a boxful of twelve different holiday cupcakes—all decorated with gingerbread men, snowflakes, and reindeer? December is also the time we break out our special holiday packaging—we have shiny silver stickers, instead of our traditional black ones, and shimmery silver ribbon—making everyone's holiday cupcakes feel a little more special!

During December, we had more than a hundred delivery orders a day and baked well over ten thousand cupcakes a day! It was Christmas chaos!

Who wouldn't love a boxful of twelve different holiday cupcakes—all decorated with gingerbread men, snowflakes, and reindeer?

Working with fondant is a lot of fun! Fondant, essentially, is a sugar dough made from confectioners' sugar, water, and corn syrup—like an edible Play-Doh. You can mold it into any shape you like and use it to decorate your cupcakes—and it's edible! Very few bakeries make their own fondant—instead most get it from special suppliers. At home, you can purchase fondant in the cake-decorating aisle of your local craft or specialty food stores. It usually comes in a small package, in various colors. We always like to work with white fondant and then add a little gel food color to achieve the exact color that we want, but you can certainly use precolored fondant too.

When working with fondant, it's important to work as quickly as possible since the fondant can dry out fast. Always keep your fondant sealed in a zip-locked bag or container when not in use.

To cut shapes out of fondant, first sprinkle some confectioners' sugar on your work surface so the fondant doesn't stick. Then, take a piece of fondant about the size of a plum and knead it with your hands until it is soft and pliable. Place the fondant on your work surface, and roll it out to a flat sheet, about ¼-inch thick, using a rolling pin. Then, using a scalpel or mini cookie cutter, cut out your desired shape! We collect mini cookie cutters in a zillion different shapes so that we can cut out any shape that we like.

Remove the cut shape from the excess fondant and place on top of your cupcake. If you'd like, you can press in small candies, nonpareils, and so forth, into the fondant to jazz up your decorations. For example, we like to add a candy center to all our fondant flowers, and red candy buttons on all our gingerbread men. ✲

Recipe for Success

Like Santa Says, Be Nice!

ome Christmastime, Santa knows who has been naughty and who has been nice, but he is not the only one! Customers, colleagues, business contacts, friends, and family also pay attention to who has been nice. Treat your colleagues and customers with respect, don't gossip about others (as this may come back to haunt you), and strive to provide the best customer service possible. Always *smile* when you are interacting with customers. Also, take the time to listen to customers if they have special requests and in particular if they have had any problems. A happy customer is a loyal customer, and it is amazing how much a smile, a polite conversation, and a willingness to hear people out can build loyalty and a connection between a customer and a store. Likewise, being nice and treating employees with respect will make them want to work hard for you. Building personal connections and creating an enjoyable experience is key to running any successful business.

Katherine's Chocolate Peppermint Hot Cocoa

One of my favorite things to do around the holidays is make hot cocoa. I love coming into the shop in the morning, when it's still dark outside, and making an amazing hot cocoa and then

settling down at the fondant table to get to work. Everyone at the shop knows about my Chocolate Peppermint Hot Cocoa, and when it is really cold outside, I make enough for the line of customers outside and we pass it out in tiny paper cups. Everyone loves it! —Katherine

Makes 4 large mugs

½ cup Callebaut chocolate chips
¼ cup heavy cream
4 cups whole milk
2 teaspoons pure peppermint extract
4 candy canes, for serving

Melt chocolate chips in heavy cream over a double boiler to make ganache. Once chips are completely melted, remove from heat. Heat the whole milk on low heat in a small saucepan. Stir in the melted ganache and stir continuously for 5 minutes until completely incorporated and before the milk comes to a boil. Add the peppermint extract and stir. Pour into four cups and garnish with candy canes.

chilling out cupcakes

Keeping cupcakes their freshest is really a science. There is only one thing you really need to remember: *never put your cupcakes in the refrigerator!* Freezing cupcakes is fine, as it retains their moisture, whereas refrigerating dries them out. When you freeze a cupcake, it locks the moisture in and freezes the chemical processes by which cupcakes dry out. Refrigerating cupcakes will *speed up* the chemical process that causes a cupcake to dry out. We always like to freeze our cupcakes in a sealed plastic container and then they can be frozen for up to two weeks. Cupcakes can be frozen after they are frosted, which is actually better, since the layer of frosting helps to lock in the moisture in the cupcake itself. Cupcakes will usually completely defrost in 2 to 3 hours, so be sure to take them out of the freezer 2 to 3 hours before you plan to serve them. After they come to room temperature, the cupcakes taste exactly the same as when they went into the freezer—moist and delicious! We use this technique to ship our cupcakes across the country. We bake, frost, and then freeze our cupcakes for 4 to 6 hours. Then we package them up and ship them overnight with a frozen ice pack so they arrive at their destination the next day still cool, fresh, beautiful, and delicious! ✱

Cheers!

When we were kids, every day at 4:00 P.M. we'd pile onto the sofa, Babee in the middle, and watch *The Oprah Winfrey Show*. Oprah was larger than life to us, a person who had done so many things for so many people and yet who had stayed true to herself. We idolized her as little girls and as young women as well. During our first few months at Georgetown Cupcake, we spent our early mornings in the bakery fantasizing about what it would be like to meet her one day. When you're working at 3:00 A.M., it's easy to get caught up in those fantasies; it's still dark outside, there are no cars on the street, and it is eerily quiet and calm except for the soft *whir* of our mixers. So we pondered,

"What if, one day, we became big enough to be on *Oprah*? What if she asked us to come on her show and bake cupcakes?"

Then one day, right before New Year's, we got the call. . . .

We were in the lab, fighting (what else is new?) over something that wasn't quite right with an order, when the phone rang. Sophie answered, and her eyes got huge and wide while she listened. A Harpo producer was calling to see if we could be on *The Oprah Winfrey Show*. We thought someone was punking us! It just didn't make sense. Us? Katherine and Sophie on *Oprah*? It finally sunk in when we each did an hour-long preinterview with the producers on the phone. It wasn't a practical joke: Oprah wanted us!

Before we could hop on the plane to Chicago, there were a million things to be done. We had to decide what we were going to bake with Oprah. We wanted to do something special and memorable, so we thought and thought and thought. Mommy chimed in with her two cents, as usual. She had been nagging us to make a cupcake parfait ever since we opened, so it was no surprise that she pitched her idea to us once again. However, this time, instead of just automatically dismissing her idea, we looked at each other and thought, *This could work here!* We came up with serving our strawberry champagne cupcakes layered with chocolate ganache in a champagne flute for New Year's Eve. It was perfect! Next, Oprah had to approve the recipe, so we FedExed the cupcakes to her. The FedEx guy came to our shop in Georgetown at 6:00 A.M. to pick them up, and they were at Harpo Studios in Chicago by noon! The official word: she loved them . . . we were on our way!

When we arrived in Chicago the day before the taping, we were ushered into a rehearsal. We were in shock when we set foot on the stage—the lights were so bright, and the studio was much smaller than it looked on TV. It felt almost homey and cozy. We practiced what we would say and do, imagining the two hundred people watching us from their seats and Oprah hovering over our shoulders. We looked at each other and nodded. We could read each other's minds: *This is it. The big time.*

The next morning was the show's taping. We arrived at the studio at 6:00 A.M. to start assembling the cupcakes for the audience. As we were putting together the two hundred cupcakes in the champagne flutes to hand out to the audience, Oprah walked past us in the hallway. "Good morning!" she said. We nearly died! She was still in her sweat suit, not yet dressed for the show—but she looked great—just like she looked on TV! Mommy was on cloud nine hanging out in the green room while we worked. We were covered in frosting when it was time to get our hair and makeup done, so we had to quickly clean up our black dresses and pink aprons. Before we knew it, we were on! Our hearts were pounding, but Oprah immediately put us at ease: she wasn't wearing any shoes behind our cooking display! She confessed that her shoes hurt too much, and it was nice to know that she had the same issues with shoes we all do. She talked to us and even held our hands before the segment started. She was so warm and supportive—and as we showed her the ingredients, her eyes lit up like a little kid in a candy store! She also looked *gorgeous* with her makeup and hair now done, and her sweat suit replaced with a pretty gray tweed sweater.

Oprah was larger than life to us, a person who had done so many things for so many people and yet who had stayed true to herself.

"You brought along a festive treat that everyone can make this New Year's Eve—I think this is great!" Oprah enthused as the cameras rolled. We showed her how we made the cupcakes and the champagne buttercream frosting, and placed them in the flutes. We diced the strawberries and demonstrated how we soak them in champagne for about ten minutes. "That's the part I like!" Oprah joked, eyeing the bubbly.

Next, we talked about how we whip up the frosting. "And there's champagne in the cupcakes *and* the frosting!" Oprah beamed at the audience. "Oh, happy day!" And when we told her how to pronounce the word *ganache,* she commented, "Heavy cream and chocolate chips! Oh, lord!"

Oprah made her own strawberry champagne cupcake parfait in the flute, adding tons of chocolate and pouring a whole cup of champagne right on top! She cracked us up. For a final touch, we put a sparkler on top and lit it. "What a nice treat for the holidays, don't you think?" Oprah asked the audience, which burst into thunderous applause. "That is simple and lovely."

As we went to the commercial break, we caught a glimpse of Mommy, beaming in the audience. What a day this was for us, and a great kickoff to a fabulous new year! Several of our recipes are now on Oprah's website (www.oprah.com), and it was a thrill to see the surge in visits to our website and the orders pour in from across the country. We also loved it when people posted photos of strawberry champagne cupcakes that they made for their own New Year's celebrations. We still have to pinch ourselves when we watch the segment (and trust us—we've watched it a million times!). I don't think Oprah has any idea how much it meant to us and what a big dream she made come true. It was a really special moment for us and something that we will always look back on as one of our proudest accomplishments.

sisters' baking secret
chocolate of choice

A lot of people ask us what chocolate they should use to make ganache. It's really a personal preference, since different chocolates have different flavor undertones—some can be fruity or spicy, others bittersweet or mild. We always like to use Valrhona and Callebaut—French and Belgian chocolates. We think they are the best. As a general rule, it is a good idea to use high-quality chocolate. Chocolate is produced in several locations all over the world, and each location's temperature, humidity, and soil quality can lead to noticeable differences in flavor. The highest-quality chocolate is usually produced in small batches with very few additional ingredients. Not sure what kind of chocolate to use? Well, here's the best part: do a taste test till you find your favorite. Yum! ✱

New Year's Eve Strawberry Champagne Sparkler Cupcakes (as seen on *The Oprah Winfrey Show*)

**Served in champagne flutes, makes 12 servings
(36 mini cupcakes: 3 per champagne flute)**

FOR THE CUPCAKES

½ cup fresh strawberries, diced

½ cup good champagne (sweet rosé
 champagne suggested)

2 ½ cups all-purpose flour

2 ½ teaspoons baking powder

¼ teaspoon salt

8 tablespoons unsalted butter (European
 style recommended)

1 ¾ cups sugar

2 large eggs, at room temperature

2 ¼ teaspoons pure vanilla extract

seeds from 1 vanilla bean

1 ¼ cups whole milk, at room temperature

FOR THE CHAMPAGNE BUTTERCREAM FROSTING

16 tablespoons unsalted butter, at room
 temperature (European style recommended)

4 cups confectioners' sugar, sifted

1 teaspoon pure vanilla extract

1 teaspoon whole milk

⅛ teaspoon salt

½ cup good champagne (sweet rosé
 champagne suggested)

FOR THE STRAWBERRY LAYER

24 fresh strawberries

1 cup good champagne (sweet rosé
 champagne suggested)

FOR THE CHOCOLATE GANACHE

2 cups high-quality semisweet chocolate chips

1 cup heavy cream

FOR SERVING

12 glass champagne flutes

12 indoor-safe sparkler candles

12 long spoons

For the cupcakes:

1 Preheat the oven to 350°F. Line two mini cupcake pans with thirty-six mini baking cups, or grease pans with butter if not using baking cups.

2 Soak the fresh strawberries in the champagne. Set aside.

3 Sift together the flour, baking powder, and salt on a sheet of parchment paper or wax paper and set aside.

4 Place the unsalted butter in the bowl of a stand mixer or in a bowl with a handheld electric mixer. Add the sugar; beat on medium speed until well incorporated.

5 Add the eggs one at a time, mixing slowly after each addition.

6 Combine the vanilla extract, vanilla bean seeds, and milk in a large liquid measuring cup.

7 Reduce the speed to low. Add one third of the flour mixture to the butter mixture, then gradually add one third of the milk mixture, beating until well incorporated. Add another third of the flour mixture, followed by one third of the milk mixture. Stop to scrape down the bowl as needed. Add the remaining flour mixture, followed by the remaining milk mixture, and mix slowly until just combined.

8 Drain the strawberries of excess champagne, and gently fold the strawberries into the batter, just until incorporated. If you are of age, the remaining champagne is a sweet treat!

9 Scoop batter into baking cups and bake for 10 minutes or until a toothpick inserted into the center of a cupcake comes out clean. Transfer the pan to a wire rack to cool completely. If using paper baking cups, peel off all the paper baking cups once the cupcakes are cool.

For the frosting:

1 Place the unsalted butter in the bowl of a stand mixer or in a bowl with a handheld electric mixer. Add the confectioners' sugar; beat on medium speed until well incorporated.

2 Add the vanilla extract, milk, salt, and champagne, and beat on high speed until light and fluffy. Place frosting in a disposable piping bag with a large round tip.

To prepare the strawberries:

Slice the strawberries lengthwise and soak in the champagne for approximately 10 to 15 minutes. Note that these strawberries should be larger slices than the ones used in the cupcakes.

For the chocolate ganache:

Fill a medium saucepan with an inch or two of water and place over medium-low heat. Place the chocolate chips and heavy cream in a medium glass bowl over the saucepan and melt the chocolate chips. Stir occasionally until the chips are completely melted. Remove the bowl of melted chocolate from the saucepan. Pour the ganache into a plastic squeeze bottle. (If a squeeze bottle is not available, you can drizzle with a spoon.)

To assemble the layers in champagne flutes:

1 Line up 12 glass champagne flutes. Insert one mini strawberry champagne cupcake in the bottom of each glass. Next, pipe a swirl of champagne buttercream frosting on top of each cupcake. Add several slices of champagne-soaked strawberries and a drizzle of chocolate ganache. Repeat layers. Finally, place a third mini strawberry champagne cupcake at the top of each glass, pipe with a final Georgetown Cupcake signature swirl (see page 23) of champagne buttercream frosting, and top with a final drizzle of chocolate ganache.

2 Insert one indoor-safe sparkler candle in the top of each glass. Light the candles at midnight, serve with spoons, and enjoy!

JANUARY 6, 1987

It was Babee's birthday—time to surprise her with a party and her favorite chocolate cake! We were ten and eight years old, and we decorated the kitchen with a HAPPY BIRTHDAY banner. Mommy kept Babee occupied in the living room while we decorated. We're sure that she knew what we were scheming, but she managed to act surprised when she walked into the kitchen and we screamed "Happy Birthday" with a chocolate cake in hand!

We, of course, used her chocolate cake recipe. We had to dig it out of the kitchen drawer where she stored it. Babee had all her recipes scribbled on crumpled lined paper, but she never referred to them and there was never a cookbook to be found. We did a very simple chocolate frosting—just melted chocolate chips and heavy cream—and poured it over the round cake. We placed strawberries along the edge and put birthday candles in the center. Every year after, this was our tradition for her birthday. As we got older, and our baking technique improved, we got a little "fancier" with her chocolate cake: we would bake two layers of chocolate cake, and spread a layer of strawberry buttercream in between the layers and frost the outside of the cake in strawberry buttercream, then line the circumference of the cake in fresh strawberries. It was beautiful!

When we first started baking, we could never remember any measurements and we would pull out Babee's recipes for reference. Now, after baking thousands upon thousands of cupcakes, we finally know every recipe by heart. We know how heavy a cup of flour is and what a teaspoon of vanilla looks like. It has become second nature to us. We don't have any recipes written down in our bakery. Everyone who bakes at Georgetown Cupcake has memorized each and every recipe. Like Babee, we bake from instinct . . . and from the heart.

Chocolate Layer Cake with Strawberry Buttercream

Makes one double-layer 9-inch round cake

FOR THE CAKE

2 ½ cups all-purpose flour

1 teaspoon baking soda

½ teaspoon salt

16 tablespoons European-style unsalted
butter, at room temperature (Plugrá brand,
recommended)

2 ½ cups sugar

4 large eggs, at room temperature

2 cups whole milk, at room temperature

2 ½ teaspoons pure vanilla extract
(preferably Madagascar Bourbon)

1 cup Valrhona cocoa powder, sifted
(may substitute another good-quality
cocoa powder)

FOR THE STRAWBERRY BUTTERCREAM
FROSTING

32 tablespoons unsalted butter,
at room temperature

8 cups confectioners' sugar,
sifted

2 teaspoons whole milk

2 teaspoons pure vanilla extract

¼ teaspoon salt

1 cup strawberries, diced and
strained

12 fresh whole strawberries,
for garnish

For the cake:

❶ Preheat the oven to 350°F and grease two 9-inch round cake pans with butter.

❷ Sift together the flour, baking soda, and salt on a piece of parchment paper or wax paper and set aside.

❸ In the bowl of a stand mixer or in a bowl with a handheld electric mixer, cream together the butter and sugar on medium for 3 to 5 minutes, or until light and fluffy.

❹ Add the eggs one at a time, mixing slowly after each addition.

5 Combine the milk and vanilla in a large liquid measuring cup.

6 Add one third of the dry ingredients, followed by one third of the milk and vanilla, and mix. Repeat. Stop to scrape down the bowl as needed. Add the last third of the dry ingredients, followed by the last third of the milk and vanilla.

7 Add the cocoa powder, mixing slowly until just incorporated.

8 Pour batter into the two greased cake pans and place in the center of the oven to bake for 30 to 35 minutes. Start checking with a toothpick at 30 minutes.

9 Let cakes cool completely (approximately 15 minutes).

For the frosting:

1 Place all ingredients except for strawberries in a stand mixer and whip for 5 minutes until the frosting is light and fluffy. Using a spatula, fold in the diced strawberries.

2 Remove the cakes from the pans. Using a serrated knife, trim off the rounded top part of each cake so the cake top is completely flat.

3 Place one cake on a plate or serving platter. Using a small offset spatula, spread a thick layer of strawberry buttercream over the cake. Place the second layer of chocolate cake on top, and then cover the top and sides with strawberry buttercream. Place fresh strawberries along the edge of the cake, all the way around, and enjoy!

Recipe for Success

Believe in Your Idea—Even If No One Else Does

From the moment we quit our jobs and filed the paperwork to formally establish Georgetown Cupcake, the clock was ticking. We would spend our days walking through the streets of Georgetown, looking at available spaces for lease. Once we found the tiny little building that would become our original shop, we had to coordinate all the renovations, including obtaining the necessary permits, locating and purchasing all the equipment and kitchen supplies we would need, setting up relationships with ingredient suppliers, and choosing all the finishes like the floors, shelving, countertops, and lighting.

As we went about this process, our savings rapidly dwindled. We decided to apply for a loan to cover some of the costs we were incurring, but each bank we approached turned us down. The loan officers had formulas telling them who should have their loan applications approved, and as a new business, we did not fit their criteria. They could not see how two young women wanting to bake cupcakes for a living could be successful in Georgetown.

We were discouraged, but undeterred. When starting a business, it is so important to believe in yourself and your idea. If you can't convince yourself that your business is viable and will be successful, it will be that much more difficult to convince banks and vendors. But if you believe in yourself, things have a funny way of working out, even if it doesn't seem like it at the time.

We ended up maxing out all of our personal credit cards and draining our bank accounts. It wasn't the ideal situation and certainly not the best way to start a business, but it was the only option we had. In the end, we told ourselves that the worst that could happen was that we would lose our savings and have to start over, and we were okay with that. We would bounce back, and would be proud with the knowledge that we had given our best effort. It would have been more of a shame to have never taken a shot at pursuing our dream.

Sweet Hearts

Valentine's Day is the biggest day of the year at Georgetown Cupcake, not only because it's the anniversary of our shop, but also because cupcakes have become a unique and special way for couples to show their love for each other. It's thrilling to see how our cupcakes have become part of the story of so many relationships. This year was one of our biggest yet.

It's always fun for us to witness the different camps of men who come into the shop on Valentine's Day. First, there are the men who plan ahead and call the shop weeks in advance to place their orders. Then, there are the men who call the shop the afternoon before Valentine's Day to place their orders last-minute. We got a call from a group of twelve men who were all sitting around a speakerphone in their office conference room the day before Valentine's Day. "Can you help us?" they pleaded. It was pretty cute! We took care of all twelve of their orders for their wives and girlfriends right then and there, and they were all quite relieved. Then, we have the frantic men who come into the shop on Valentine's Day and pick out their cupcakes on the spot. We wrap them with a beautiful bow . . . so their loved ones never know they procrastinated, or worse, nearly forgot about Valentine's Day altogether.

In addition, each year, lots of male customers contact us to discuss how to propose to their girlfriend using cupcakes. One of the most popular ways is to spell out the question "Will you marry me?" on top of cupcakes. But this year we had an extra-special proposal on Valentine's Day. A gentleman called the shop and explained what he wanted to do: propose in the shop, on Valentine's Day, at closing, when it was quiet, and surprise his girlfriend by placing the ring in the frosting of a Red Velvet cupcake. So, instead of a fondant heart, there would be a diamond floating on top of the icing! Naturally, we loved this idea—and we're suckers for romance.

We held a table for them at 8:45 P.M., and he came into the office early to give us the ring so we could frost a fresh Red Velvet cupcake, place the beautiful diamond

solitaire in the icing, and gift-wrap it in a single pink box. When the shop cleared out of customers, all of us huddled in the back, waiting for them to have their moment. After she said yes, we all jumped out and took a picture with the happy couple! She was floored and thrilled!

sisters' baking secret
how we survive valentine's day!

Our prep for the holiday actually starts several weeks before, as advance orders start to pile up. We have to create special-order binders just for the day, one binder each for delivery and pickup orders, and also arrange special deliveries of ribbon, packaging supplies, and ingredients. The night before, we organize all the orders by time window and clip gift notes and pickup or delivery slips to each order form. By the time we are ready to close up for the night, the early baking shift is showing up to start!

At 3:00 A.M., the packing starts. After grabbing a couple hours of sleep, we bundle up, head into the shop, and get started on packing the morning deliveries, which sometimes number in the hundreds. The best part is reading all the gift notes, which range from a simple and traditional "Happy Valentine's Day" to the most heartfelt and romantic personal messages from husbands who are out of town or deployed overseas and sending cupcakes to their wives and daughters. It is so heartwarming to play even a small part in making this day special. It's a little like being Cupid!

Around one hour before opening, after many of our staff have already worked a full day, the line of customers starts to form outside. By the time we open, the line extends all the way down the block, and it stays that way the whole day. The actual workday is a blur, a constant stream of customers ordering cupcakes several dozen at a time. Even with a ten-hour head start, the cupcakes fly out the door almost as quickly as we can bake them. The phones are ringing constantly.

Even with all the activity in the shop, the mood is light and cheery and the customers are all smiling. There is just something about Valentine's Day that has made it about more than chocolate and flowers and candy hearts; it has become a day for showing the people one loves how special they are, and cupcakes are a fun, creative, and delicious way to make the message personal. ✪

Georgetown Cupcake Red Velvet Cupcakes

Ever since we were little girls, we loved Valentine's Day. We remember exchanging valentines with our classmates; our favorites were the scratch-and-sniff ones. We also loved the red hot candy hearts—we would eat so many that our tongues would burn and turn bright red! But most of all, we loved baking Red Velvet cupcakes for Valentine's Day with sweet cream-cheese frosting piled high on top.

Red Velvet is our most popular cupcake flavor year-round—but on Valentine's Day, we bake an *extra* crazy amount of Red Velvet. There's something romantic about Red Velvet. The cupcakes themselves have a gorgeous red hue, and we top them with our signature swirl of light and airy vanilla cream-cheese frosting and a tiny red fondant heart brushed with edible luster dust. When we look at them all lined up on a tray, they look so sweet and delicate, with just a touch of shimmer.

Makes 12 cupcakes

FOR THE CUPCAKES

3 ¼ cups all-purpose flour

1 teaspoon salt

12 tablespoons unsalted butter, at room temperature (European style recommended)

1 ¾ cups sugar

2 large eggs, at room temperature

4 tablespoons red food color (no-taste liquid food color, such as McCormick)

1 teaspoon pure vanilla extract (Madagascar Bourbon recommended)

2 ½ tablespoons cocoa powder, sifted (such as Valrhona)

1 ½ cups whole milk, at room temperature

1 ½ teaspoons baking soda

1 ½ teaspoons apple cider vinegar

FOR THE VANILLA CREAM-CHEESE FROSTING

See recipe, page 20.

For the cupcakes:

1 Preheat the oven to 350°F. Line a standard cupcake pan with twelve paper baking cups, or grease the pan with butter if not using baking cups.

2 Sift together the flour and salt, and set aside.

3 In the bowl of a stand mixer or in a bowl with a handheld electric mixer, cream together the butter and sugar at medium speed for 3 to 5 minutes, or until light and fluffy.

4 Add the eggs one at a time, mixing slowly after each addition.

5 Using a whisk, whisk together the red food color, vanilla, and cocoa powder. Slowly add this to the mixer bowl, mixing slowly until well incorporated.

6 Add one third of the flour, followed by one third of the milk, and mix. Repeat. Stop to scrape down the bowl as needed. Add the last third of the flour, followed by the last third of the milk, and mix until incorporated.

7 In a small bowl, add the baking soda to the apple cider vinegar. You will see the baking soda and vinegar fizz up! Mix thoroughly and add this reaction to the batter. Mix until just incorporated.

8 Using a standard-size ice-cream scoop, scoop the batter into a cupcake pan so each well is two-thirds full. Bake for 16 to 18 minutes (start checking at 15 minutes) or until a toothpick comes out clean. Transfer the pan to a wire rack to cool completely.

For the frosting:

See recipe, page 20. Frost each cupcake with a signature swirl of frosting (see page 23) and top with a fondant red heart.

sisters' baking secret
a variety of vanillas

There are three main types of vanilla: Madagascar Bourbon is rich and sweet, has the strongest vanilla flavor, and is the one we use in our baking; Tahitian has a fruity, floral flavor; and Mexican has a spicy flavor. It's a personal choice, of course. Experiment to see which flavor you like the most. If you really want to amp up the vanilla flavor in your cupcakes, try scraping the seeds out of a vanilla bean pod and adding it to your batter or icing. Not only does it give the vanilla flavor an extra kick, but also the specks of vanilla bean seeds in your cupcakes or frosting look beautiful. We still like to use the liquid extract in addition to the seeds, but you can try different variations to see which one you like best. ✱

Recipe for Success

Love What You Do

*S*uccessful people all have one thing in common: they like what they do. Have you ever heard of a thriving business owner grumble that he hates coming to work every day? Of course not; he's tapped into his passion and drive. Having a passion for your work not only makes you more productive, but your positive feelings rub off on your colleagues, customers, family, and friends. This is especially true if you start your own business. Being an entrepreneur is not easy, as we have said. Nor is it a nine-to-five job. The only way you can put in the time, effort, and dedication it takes is to really love the job. So what if you have no idea what it is you love to do?

What if you have no clue where your passion lies? It's not always so easy to figure out; it can take time and a lot of patience, as well as trial and error. Ask yourself how you spend your time off: What hobbies do you have? Where do you go? Do you like working and interacting with people all the time, or do you prefer honing in on a specific project and solving problems on your own? Sometimes, it helps to figure out what you *don't* like doing first; that can eventually lead you to what you *do* like. We are very fortunate to be able to do what we love every day, and do it alongside the people we care about most. The days fly by, the work is incredibly rewarding, and most of all, it's fun.

Sophie and Katherine's Chocolate Truffles

Another thing we love to make on Valentine's Day is chocolates. Our favorites are these chocolate truffles, which you can coat with your favorite toppings, and they are really easy to make at home.

Makes 24 chocolate truffles

36 ounces good-quality chocolate chips (Callebaut or Valrhona recommended), separated

8 tablespoons unsalted butter, at room temperature

1 cup heavy cream

2 tablespoons corn syrup

2 cups chopped hazelnuts, shredded coconut, chocolate sprinkles, or your favorite topping

❶ Melt 24 ounces of chocolate chips with the butter in a glass bowl over a double boiler and stir until smooth.

❷ In a separate small pot, heat the heavy cream and corn syrup over medium-high heat for 5 to 6 minutes. Remove from the heat and add to the bowl with the melted chocolate and butter. Mix thoroughly and cover with plastic wrap. Refrigerate for 45 minutes to an hour, or until the chocolate reaches the consistency of peanut butter.

❸ Using a mini ice-cream scoop, scoop small chunks of chilled chocolate and line them up on a baking sheet. Once all chocolate is scooped out, chill in the refrigerator for 15 to 20 minutes, for the chunks to harden.

❹ Melt the remaining 12 ounces of chocolate over a double boiler and let cool slightly. Pour toasted hazelnuts or a topping of your choice in a shallow pan or dish.

❺ Remove chilled chocolate chunks from the refrigerator and shape the chunks into round balls or the shape of your choice.

6 Using a toothpick, dip the truffle into the cooled melted chocolate, and then roll it and coat it in the topping. Let the topping set on each truffle, approximately 20 minutes, then serve at room temperature or chilled.

Part 3

SPRING

We love when the frost melts away and the flowers and trees begin to bloom again. Spring is the perfect time to stop, smell the fragrant blossoms, and appreciate the sweet, simple things in life.

Birthdays and Hummingbirds

The first cake that Sophie and I ever baked was for my grandfather. It was a vanilla cake with a milk chocolate buttercream frosting for his birthday. I can still remember making that cake, even though I was barely four years old at the time. I was Sophie's sous chef, following all her orders in the kitchen. Not much has changed since then! There was a wonderful simplicity to that cake. I remember using the handheld beater to mix the eggs, which made a beautiful yellow cake. And I remember slathering the milk chocolate buttercream frosting onto its rectangular shape. We posed for a picture with that cake; we were so proud of what we had accomplished on our own. Papou and Babee loved the cake so much, they hung that picture on their kitchen wall.

I was born on the same day as my grandfather, March 13, and that gave us a very strong bond from the beginning (sometimes I think he favored me just a little because of it!). He was a true gentleman and a role model for Sophie and me growing up. We both looked up to him in so many ways. He had left his home country of Greece to provide a better life for his family in Canada. He was very brave to move to a country where he didn't speak the language and didn't know a soul. He learned to speak English and got a job at an engineering company and slowly worked his way up. He was a true risk taker; I guess that's where Sophie and I get it from!

Papou always said that by working hard you could accomplish anything you wanted. I think that through his example, we believed, sometimes naively, that Papou was right. His work ethic was really strong, but his love for his family was even stronger. I remember him letting us work with him in the garden, helping him pick the grapes to make his homemade wine. He trusted us to take on a lot of responsibilities at a young age, like pruning the trees and collecting and bundling the branches to be taken away. He took great measures to make sure that his yard was perfect. Each tree was expertly pruned, the rose bushes were properly tended to, and the garden was in perfect order, with rows upon rows of straight pepper and tomato plants with trenches between them so they would be properly watered. He raised us to be strong, take-charge, independent individuals.

Our grandfather died at age eighty-three, just after our shared birthday. Every year, whenever I blow out the candle on a milk chocolate birthday cupcake, I think of him doing it with me. I miss him every single day—not just on our birthday—and I treasure the memories we made together. —Katherine

Milk Chocolate Birthday Cupcakes

Makes 12 cupcakes

FOR THE CUPCAKES

2 ½ cups all-purpose flour

2 ½ teaspoons baking powder

¼ teaspoon salt

8 tablespoons unsalted butter, at room
   temperature (European style recommended)

1 ¾ cups sugar

2 large eggs, at room temperature

2 ¼ teaspoons pure vanilla extract

seeds from 1 vanilla bean

1 ¼ cups whole milk, at room temperature

FOR MILK CHOCOLATE
BUTTERCREAM FROSTING

⅔ cup milk, at room temperature

5 cups confectioners' sugar

12 tablespoons butter, at room
   temperature

5 teaspoons pure vanilla extract

½ teaspoon salt

2 ½ cups chocolate chips, melted and then
   cooled to room temperature

rainbow sprinkles (optional)

For the cupcakes:

❶ Preheat the oven to 350°F. Line a standard cupcake pan with twelve paper baking cups, or grease the pan with butter if not using baking cups.

❷ Sift together the flour, baking powder, and salt on a sheet of parchment paper or wax paper and set aside.

❸ In the bowl of a stand mixer or in a bowl with a handheld electric mixer, cream together the butter and sugar for 3 to 5 minutes, or until light and fluffy.

❹ Add the eggs one at a time, mixing slowly after each addition.

❺ Add the vanilla and vanilla bean seeds to the milk in a large liquid measuring cup.

6 Add one third of the dry ingredients followed by one third of the milk, and mix thoroughly. Repeat. Stop to scrape down the bowl as needed. Add the last third of the dry ingredients followed by the last third of the milk, mixing slowly until well incorporated.

7 Scoop the batter into the cupcake pan using a standard-size ice-cream scoop and bake for 16 to 18 minutes (start checking at 15 minutes) or until a toothpick comes out clean. Transfer the pan to a wire rack to cool completely.

For the frosting:

1 Combine the milk, confectioners' sugar, butter, vanilla, and salt at high speed until light and airy, approximately 3 to 5 minutes. Slowly add the melted chocolate until well incorporated.

2 Frost using the signature swirl (see page 23)! Top with rainbow sprinkles if desired.

Recipe for Success

Don't Let an Argument Come Between You

That was Papou's message to us every time we would fight as little girls. Too often, siblings grow apart, friends stop talking, business partners differ and split. Papou made us see that most of our bickering was over something silly or insignificant; he helped us keep things in perspective. It's a valuable lesson for any relationship, personal or professional: don't let an argument tear you apart. If you give yourselves some time to cool off, and try and see through the other person's eyes, usually you'll realize that the battle is not such a big deal. We might argue, we might tattle to Mommy when one of us is being a pain, but we love each other as only sisters can—and nothing will ever change that.

Irish Cream Cupcakes

As kids, every St. Patrick's Day, our grandmother would dress us up head to toe in green. In retrospect, it's pretty funny since our grandparents were very Greek and probably didn't understand what the heck everyone was celebrating on this day. We think it was their way of assimilating into their new cultural surroundings.

During the day, we would run out into their backyard, dressed in our green slacks and shirts, and drop to the ground, searching for four-leaf clovers amid the grass. Our grandfather had found one years back and always kept it in his wallet to show us. He said it brought him good luck. We desperately wanted to find one on our own to bring us good luck, too, and would spend hours going through blades of grass to see who could get their hands on one first.

We never did find a four-leaf clover all those years. Now we believe you make your own luck in life!

Makes 18 cupcakes

FOR THE CUPCAKES

1 ¼ cups all-purpose flour

½ teaspoon baking soda

¼ teaspoon salt

8 tablespoons European-style unsalted butter, at room temperature

1 ¼ cups sugar

2 large eggs, at room temperature

1 ¼ teaspoons pure vanilla extract (preferably Madagascar Bourbon)

1 cup whole milk, at room temperature

½ cup Valrhona cocoa powder, sifted (may substitute another good-quality cocoa powder)

½ cup Irish Cream (such as Bailey's brand or nonalcoholic Irish Cream coffee syrup)

FOR THE IRISH CREAM FROSTING

4 tablespoons unsalted butter, at room temperature

4 cups confectioners' sugar, sifted

¼ teaspoon pure vanilla extract

6 ounces cream cheese, at room temperature

¼ cup Irish Cream (such as Bailey's brand or nonalcoholic Irish Cream coffee syrup)

For the cupcakes:

1 Preheat the oven to 350°F. Line a standard cupcake pan with twelve paper baking cups, and a second pan with six baking cups, or grease pans with butter if not using baking cups.

2 Sift together the flour, baking soda, and salt on a sheet of parchment paper or wax paper and set aside.

3 Place the butter in the bowl of a stand mixer or in a bowl with a handheld electric mixer. Beat on medium speed until fluffy. Stop to add the sugar; then beat on medium

speed until well incorporated. Add the eggs one at a time, mixing slowly after each addition.

4 Combine the vanilla extract and milk in a large liquid measuring cup.

5 Reduce the speed to low. Add one third of the flour mixture to the butter mixture, then gradually add one third of the milk mixture, beating until well incorporated. Add another third of the flour mixture, followed by one third of the milk mixture. Stop to scrape down the bowl as needed. Add the remaining flour mixture, followed by the remaining milk mixture, and mix slowly until just combined.

6 Add the cocoa powder, beating on low speed until just incorporated.

7 Add the Irish Cream, still beating on low speed, until just incorporated.

8 Use a standard-size ice-cream scoop to fill each baking cup with batter, so that the wells are two-thirds full. Bake for 18 to 20 minutes (start checking at 15 minutes) or until a toothpick inserted into the center of a cupcake comes out clean. Transfer the pan to a wire rack to cool completely.

For the frosting:

Mix all ingredients in an electric mixer for approximately 5 minutes, until the frosting is light and airy. The Irish Cream will give the frosting a slightly beige color. When frosting the cupcakes, remember the signature swirl (see page 23)!

Hummingbird Cupcakes

There is a Greek superstition where on the first of March, mothers and grandmothers braid bracelets called Martis from red and white string for their children. Babee would tie these bracelets onto our wrists every March 1. Different villages and islands in Greece have variations of this superstition, but the bracelets are supposed to protect you from the sun of the spring so it doesn't burn your cheeks—and the red and white strings symbolize healthy pink cheeks. We would wear the bracelets until Easter Sunday and then leave them outside for the birds to use for their nests, supposedly bringing us good luck for the spring. The tradition reminds us of our Hummingbird cupcakes. Though a traditional Southern cupcake—named for the birds that drink sweet nectar—we like to think of the birds decorating their nests with Martis strings. We made this recipe with Martha Stewart on her show!

Makes 12 cupcakes

FOR THE CUPCAKES

1 ¼ cups all-purpose flour

1 ½ teaspoons baking powder

1 teaspoon ground cinnamon

¼ teaspoon ground nutmeg

¼ teaspoon salt

8 tablespoons unsalted butter, at room temperature

1 cup sugar

2 eggs, at room temperature

1 cup mashed ripe bananas (approximately 3 large bananas)

1 tablespoon clover honey

½ cup crushed pineapple, drained

½ cup chopped pecans

¼ cup hot water

For the cupcakes:

1 Preheat the oven to 350°F. Line a standard cupcake pan with twelve baking cups, or grease the pan with butter if not using baking cups.

2 Sift together the flour, baking powder, cinnamon, nutmeg, and salt on a sheet of parchment paper or wax paper and set aside.

3 Place the butter in the bowl of a stand mixer or in a bowl with a handheld electric mixer. Beat on medium speed until fluffy. Stop to add the sugar; beat on medium speed and cream together until well incorporated, approximately 2 to 3 minutes.

4 Add the eggs one at a time, mixing slowly after each addition.

5 Add the mashed bananas and honey and mix slowly to incorporate.

6 Add the pineapple, and mix slowly to incorporate.

7 Add the pecans, and mix slowly to incorporate.

8 Reduce the speed to low. Add one third of the flour mixture to the butter mixture, then gradually add one third of the hot water, beating until well incorporated. Add another third of the flour mixture, followed by one third of the hot water. Stop to scrape down the bowl as needed. Add the remaining flour mixture, followed by the remaining hot water, and mix slowly until just combined. Take care not to overmix the batter.

9 Use a standard-size ice-cream scoop to fill each baking cup with batter, so that the wells are two-thirds full. Bake for 24 to 26 minutes (start checking at 24 minutes) or until a toothpick inserted into the center of a cupcake comes out clean. Transfer the pan to a wire rack to cool completely.

For the frosting:

See recipe, page 20.

For the decoration:

1 Line up the cooled cupcakes on a counter.

2 Transfer the vanilla cream-cheese frosting into a plastic piping bag fitted with a large round metal tip.

3 Apply a signature swirl of frosting on top of each cupcake (see page 23).

4 Knead a small amount of blue (or color of your choice) gel food color into a piece of white fondant to achieve a light blue color. Using a rolling pin, roll out a thin sheet of fondant about ¼-inch thick. Dust with edible luster dust (optional). Using a mini bird-shaped cookie cutter, cut out fondant hummingbirds. Let fondant harden for 2 to 3 minutes.

5 Form a small pile of chopped pecans on each cupcake, and place a fondant hummingbird in each "nest" of pecans.

sisters' baking secret
yummy hues

The best way to color buttercream is using a few small drops of no-taste gel food color. Better to put in too little first and blend it—you can always add more if the color isn't deep enough. It's like being an artist, mixing up your colors. We find that gels don't thin out the frosting either. We always use "no-taste" color since sometimes food color can have a bitter taste to it. ✸

Beautiful Blooms and Easter Baking

APRIL 1990

In back of our grandparents' house on Oakland Drive, there were several different kinds of fruit trees: pear, apple, apricot, plum, and cherry. They were beautiful and had the sweetest, most delicious fruit. The trees were a source of pride for Papou, who would diligently tend to them every day. It was the cherry tree, though, that we were most obsessed with. It was one of the oldest trees in the neighborhood, with a very thick trunk and aged branches. It grew in the middle of the yard, directly behind the grapevine-covered patio and beside the garden. If we stood up in the tree and reached out far enough, we could touch Babee's clothesline that ran diagonally across the backyard.

In April, the tree would change almost overnight; one day the branches would be bare, and the following day we could see small, white buds begin to form on the maze of branches weaving their way into the sky. The buds would quickly turn into blossoms that showered the backyard in the most gorgeous display. They were shades of white and pink and looked so fluffy—almost like cotton candy hanging heavily on the branches.

When we were twelve and thirteen, the cherry tree was no longer just a place to play—it suddenly became our Sisters' Secret Clubhouse. We would scamper up the tree, hoist ourselves up, and carefully inch along until we reached the flat notches on the branch where we could sit comfortably and peer down into the backyard below. With the tree in full bloom, we used to think that we could hide from the world and have our own secret conversations. We would tell each other stories and laugh, discussing our family, our friends at school, and the gross boys we would never admit to liking, even if we secretly had a crush on them. One day, Babee came out to look for us and she called out in the backyard. We didn't want to reveal this magical hiding place, so we stayed completely quiet. Amazingly, the cherry blossoms provided enough cover to keep us hidden from view. Babee went back into the house, and we remained in our hideaway, giggling and sharing more secrets.

> *Blossoms showered the backyard. They were shades of white and pink and looked so fluffy—almost like cotton candy.*

Cherry Blossom Cupcakes

When we moved to Washington, DC, more than ten years ago, we had heard of the Cherry Blossom festival and how the nation's capital was famous for these beautiful cherry trees that would bloom in unison along the Tidal Basin. While we had wonderful memories of the cherry tree in our grandparents' backyard, we were amazed when we saw firsthand how breathtaking the cherry blossoms in DC were. The trees would line the basin and the entire length of the

Potomac River with their beautiful blossoms. Each tree was unique: some with magnificent displays of bold pink blossoms and others with soft, delicate white blossoms. Their branches each carved their own special pattern against the Washington skyline.

The most amazing aspect of the cherry blossoms is their fragility. Each year around late February or early March, the conversations start around town: "When will the blossoms peak?" Residents and tourists alike start planning their calendars around the peak blossom period, which typically only lasts for a few days. So many factors can change the blossoms' schedule, from a really cold day, to heavy winds, to driving rain. But for a brief period, Washington is adorned in the blossoms' majesty. We wanted to capture this beauty in one of our cupcakes. It had to be a flavor that felt light and springlike, so it's baked with fresh cherries, topped with a cloud of light and airy cherry-infused buttercream frosting, and decorated with light pink fondant cherry blossoms.

FOR THE CUPCAKES

2 ½ cups all-purpose flour

2 ½ teaspoons baking powder

¼ teaspoon salt

8 tablespoons unsalted butter, at room
temperature

1 ¾ cups sugar

2 large eggs, at room temperature

2 ¼ teaspoons pure vanilla extract

seeds from 1 vanilla bean

1 ¼ cups whole milk, at room temperature

½ cup fresh cherries, chopped (or frozen
and defrosted if fresh not available)

FOR THE CHERRY BUTTERCREAM FROSTING

16 tablespoons unsalted butter, at room
temperature

4 cups confectioners' sugar, sifted

1 teaspoon whole milk

1 teaspoon pure vanilla extract

⅛ teaspoon salt

¼ cup fresh cherry juice (juice squeezed from
cherries; if you use frozen cherries, there
should be enough juice once the cherries
have thawed)

FOR THE DECORATION

pink fondant

mini flower cookie cutter

white candy baubles (optional)

For the cupcakes:

1 Preheat the oven to 350°F. Line a standard cupcake pan with twelve paper baking cups, or grease the pan with butter if not using baking cups.

2 Sift together the flour, baking powder, and salt on parchment or wax paper and set aside.

3 In the bowl of a stand mixer or in a bowl with a handheld electric mixer, cream together the butter and sugar for 3 to 5 minutes, or until light and fluffy. Add the eggs one at a time, mixing slowly after each addition.

4 Add the vanilla extract and vanilla bean seeds to the milk in a large liquid measuring cup.

5 Add one third of the dry ingredients followed by one third of the milk, and mix thoroughly. Repeat. Stop to scrape down the bowl as needed. Add the last third of dry ingredients followed by the last third of milk. Mix slowly until just incorporated. Using a spatula, gently fold in the cherries.

6 Scoop the batter into the cupcake pan using a standard-size ice-cream scoop. Bake for 16 to 18 minutes (start checking at 15 minutes) or until a toothpick comes out clean. Transfer the pan to a wire rack to cool completely.

For the frosting:

Combine the ingredients in a mixer and whip together at high speed until light and airy, approximately 3 to 5 minutes. Load the frosting into a large piping bag with a large tip and frost each cupcake with Georgetown Cupcake's signature swirl of icing (see page 23).

For the decoration:

Roll out the pink fondant, and cut out cherry blossoms using a mini flower cookie cutter. If desired, press a candy bauble into the center of the flower. Place a flower on top of each frosted cupcake.

EASTER 1995

The night before Easter was always the longest church service of the year at our Greek Orthodox church—so we knew we were in for at least six hours straight. We were sixteen and seventeen years old, wearing the beautiful matching Easter dresses, hats, and purses Babee had bought us—all in matching lavender and pink and mint green.

When we arrived at church around 9:00 P.M., it was already filled with people. Shortly before midnight, the entire church went dark and silent, and it filled with a sense of anticipation. At midnight, the priest emerged from behind the altar with a single candle, lit against the total darkness of the church. Everyone was holding a candle, and as the priest lit one of the candles in the front row, each person in turn passed the flame to the next person. Slowly the darkness of the church was overtaken by a wave of light. As our candles were lit, we said, "Christos Anesti," which means "Christ has risen" in Greek. The entire church sang in unison, and the singing spilled outside as we all carried our lit candles out beneath the midnight sky. It was magical.

Recipe for Success

Spring Is a Time to Start Fresh

*K*okkina avga is a Greek Easter tradition that Babee always followed. She would dye eggs a deep red, symbolizing rebirth. We love this tradition and the idea that spring affords us all a time to breathe new life into our days. It's an especially energizing and exciting time in the bakery. We fill our displays with Easter cupcakes frosted to look like grass and decorated with playful fondant bunnies and flowers. Enjoy this time of year; let it put a "spring" in your step and rekindle your creativity and joy. Now is the time to stop and smell the fragrant flowers and appreciate that you can start anew.

Babee's Easter Bread

Easter was a big baking holiday in our family. Babee would start baking for Easter three days in advance and would take over both her upstairs and downstairs kitchens baking for the holiday. The most important thing she baked for the Sunday feast was her traditional Greek Easter bread. Our favorite part was helping her brush the egg wash on the loaves.

Makes one large loaf

¾ tablespoon dry yeast

¼ cup whole milk (warmed in microwave for 30 seconds)

4 cups all-purpose flour, sifted

¼ teaspoon salt

4 tablespoons unsalted butter, melted (European style recommended)

¼ tablespoon anise

juice and zest of 1 orange

½ cup water

2 eggs, at room temperature

¼ teaspoon mastic (a Greek spice, available in specialty food stores or the international aisle of supermarkets; you can make this bread without mastic)

¼ cup sugar

1 egg lightly beaten with ¼ cup water (for egg wash)

¼ cup sesame seeds

❶ Dissolve the yeast in the warmed milk. Cover and set aside in a warm place to rise for 15 minutes.

❷ In the bowl of an electric mixer, using the paddle attachment, mix together the flour, salt, and melted butter. Add the anise, orange juice, zest, and water. Mix together.

❸ Add the eggs one at a time, and mix. Then add the mastic, sugar, and the risen yeast mixture. Mix together.

❹ Using the dough hook attachment of your electric mixer (or your hands), knead the

mixture for approximately 10 minutes. Cover the bowl and allow to rise in a warm place (e.g., an oven heated to 200°F) until the dough doubles in size, approximately 2 hours.

5 Remove the dough from the bowl and beat it down to deflate it. Then, separate the dough into three pieces and roll out each piece lengthwise about one foot long. Braid the three pieces together.

6 Place the dough in a greased large loaf pan (5x10-inch pan recommended—or you can use a greased cookie sheet). Place back in warm oven and allow the dough to double in size again, approximately an hour.

7 Brush with egg wash using a pastry brush and sprinkle sesame seeds on top.

8 Preheat the oven to 350°F, then bake the bread for approximately 30 minutes, or until the top turns a golden brown.

Mommy!

Growing up, we thought we had the coolest mom. While our cousins had rules and bedtimes and had to finish their dinner before they could have dessert, we didn't. When we had sleepovers with cousins or friends, Mommy would make popcorn for us at two in the morning. Instead of going wild with a lack of rules, we respected our mother for trusting us. We finished all our homework, went to bed at a reasonable hour, and woke up early in the morning—without being nagged to do so. Most kids had to beg their mother for toys or sweet treats. Not us. If we passed an ice-cream truck, Mommy would ask, "What flavor does everyone want?" And she would always pick out the coolest toys and Barbies and surprise us with them. We suspect it's be-

> *Mommy empowered us— and she still does.*

cause, deep down, Mommy has always been a kid at heart and took pleasure in having those things for herself, too!

She wanted us to be responsible and proud, and she knew that allowing us to make our own decisions was the only way we would learn right from wrong. Mommy empowered us—and she still does. We think she's a saint!

We really put her through the wringer when we started our bakery. She came to help out on our opening weekend and we never let her leave. By this Mother's Day, we appreciated her not just for being a nurturing, devoted mom, but for being a valuable member of Georgetown Cupcake—one that we couldn't function without! She made sure that the quality of our cupcakes was consistently excellent, and she was never afraid to speak her mind and let us know if something needed to improve or change. Though we may not always tell her every day, we will always be grateful for everything she has done for us. Our shop would never have survived without her.

Mommy is now a fixture at Georgetown Cupcake—and a regular on *DC Cupcakes*. Lots of people shout, "Mommy!" when they spot her at the counter or hovering in the bakery's open kitchen, and this gives us a great thrill. Our mother has always been our biggest fan, so we're glad she has her own fan club now, too. Not that she ever expected this—she had no idea how much her life would change that first weekend. She went from a retired mother of two, enjoying her time off relaxing with our father, to working harder than she had ever worked in her entire life.

Since our grandmother passed away, our relationship with Mommy has gotten even closer. We do everything together, from watching TV and cooking to shopping and going to the spa. Some people find it so strange that we would rather hang out with our mom than with our friends, but that's truly how we feel. She is and always will be the person who can put things in perspective for us and remind us where we came from. She keeps our feet firmly planted on the ground, and she's the very first person we want to run to, whether it's with good news or a crisis!

Recipe for Success

How to Raise Strong Women

$\mathcal{W}$e are who we are today because of Mommy. So we asked her for her advice on how to be a great mom (we know we'll need it someday!).

- **Be a cheerleader.** I cherish every moment that I can cheer my girls on and jump for joy when they accomplish their goals. I have been blown away by their persistence in everything they do. But occasionally they get discouraged and I step in to remind them they can do it. Then when they do, I applaud louder than anyone.

- **Give them space.** I really tried to let my girls spread their wings and fly—and not meddle too much. I think that's what allowed them to take the risks they did and go after their dream. They know I have my opinions—and will often share them—but I leave it up to them to make the final decision.

- **Trust their instincts.** When Sophie and Katherine told me they planned to open a cupcake bakery, I didn't discourage them, but they knew I was worried. I decided to trust them with their decision to make this huge change in their lives. It was difficult in the beginning, watching them work so hard and struggle with the unknown ahead. But I knew they wanted it and believed in it, and that was enough for me.

- **Teach them to have faith.** I know Sophie and Katherine love what they are doing and that in God's grand scheme of things, they are where they should be. Sometimes you aren't sure of your path, but you have to have faith that, if you're following your heart and your dreams, you won't lose your way. —Mommy

Lemon Blueberry Cupcakes with a Citrus Glaze

This is Mommy's favorite cupcake!

Makes 12 cupcakes

FOR THE CUPCAKES

2 ½ cups all-purpose flour

2 ½ teaspoons baking powder

¼ teaspoon salt

1 ¼ cups whole milk, at room temperature

2 ¼ teaspoons pure vanilla extract

8 tablespoons unsalted butter, at room
temperature

1 ¾ cups sugar

2 large eggs, at room temperature

juice and zest from 2 lemons

½ cup fresh blueberries (or frozen if you
can't find fresh)

FOR THE CITRUS GLAZE

1 ¼ cups confectioners' sugar, sifted

½ teaspoon lemon zest

3 tablespoons freshly squeezed lemon juice

¼ teaspoon vanilla extract

For the cupcakes:

1 Preheat the oven to 350°F. Line a cupcake pan with twelve paper baking cups, or grease the pan with butter if not using baking cups.

2 Sift together the flour, baking powder, and salt on a sheet of parchment paper or wax paper and set aside.

3 Combine the milk and vanilla extract in a large liquid measuring cup.

4 In the bowl of a stand mixer or in a bowl with a handheld electric mixer, cream together the butter and sugar for 3 to 5 minutes, until it is light and fluffy.

5 Add the eggs one at a time, mixing slowly after each addition.

6 Slowly add one third of the dry ingredients followed by one third of the milk mixture. Mix slowly, and then add another third of the dry ingredients, followed by one third of the milk. Mix slowly until incorporated. Stop to scrape down the bowl as needed. Then, finally, add the last third of the dry ingredients, followed by the last third of the milk. Mix slowly until fully incorporated.

7 Add the lemon juice and lemon zest, and mix slowly.

8 Using a spatula, gently fold the blueberries into the batter.

9 Using a standard-size ice-cream scoop, scoop the batter into the cupcake pan until each well is two-thirds full and bake for 16 to 18 minutes (start checking at 15 minutes).

10 Transfer the pan to a wire rack to cool completely.

For the citrus glaze:

1 Whisk together the confectioners' sugar, lemon zest, lemon juice, and vanilla extract in a small bowl, and heat in a small saucepan on low heat until fully incorporated. Let cool for 10 minutes.

2 Pour glaze over each cupcake and enjoy!

Mommy's Mint Lemonade

Mommy has this problem throwing things away. She's not a hoarder, but she is always trying to find a use for things in the bakery—even stuff we've tossed out! Mommy hates to waste food, so she likes to use all the zested, unsqueezed lemons to make lemonade for everyone in the bakery. She can't bear to throw them out with all that wonderful juice inside. Everyone in the bakery *loves* Mommy's lemonade. She's usually in the back making some . . . when she should be doing something else! She likes to make it at especially busy times, which sometimes stresses us out . . . but then we have yummy lemonade to enjoy, so we really can't get that mad at her. This lemonade goes great with our Lemon Blueberry cupcakes and makes a wonderful pairing for a spring brunch or garden party.

1 ⅓ cups sugar

⅓ cup boiling water

2 cups freshly squeezed lemon juice

6 cups cold water

6 tablespoons crushed (chopped) fresh mint
  leaves

Dissolve all the sugar in the boiling water. Add the lemon juice, cold water, and crushed mint leaves and stir! You can garnish the glasses with a fresh lemon slice, a couple of fresh mint leaves, or both.

Part 4

SUMMER

When we were kids, we counted down the days until summer vacation: no teachers, no schedules, no homework! It was just endless fun, riding our bicycles, going for walks, running through the sprinkler, and hanging out with our family. Today, we still revel in the relaxing sunshine of summer. Nothing beats sitting on lawn chairs in our backyard during the sunny summer months, sunglasses on, soaking in the rays.

Vacation Time!

Our family didn't go on extravagant vacations off to tropical destinations for summer break when we were kids. Instead, we had two kinds of summer vacations. If we stayed locally, we would pack up our 1970s station wagon and head for the Finger Lakes in upstate New York. Or, if we had more time, we would fly to Greece to visit with our dad's family and our grandmother, Baba Domna. This was not the Greece of postcards with sunny islands and beautiful views. Instead, we would stay in a tiny little village in northern Greece without air conditioning or running water!

In June 1985, we were fortunate to take both vacations in the same year. Visiting upstate New York was our most frequent picnic vacation destination. The back of the

Picnic in upstate New York, 1981

car would be piled high with coolers full of fresh pasta and potato salads, soda bottles, and meat that we would grill. We could barely see out the back window.

We would park our station wagon at a campsite near the lake and then run around, kick a soccer ball, and play hide and seek, while Mommy set the picnic table for an amazing meal. Our father would fire up the charcoal barbecue and cook up hamburgers, hot dogs, and chicken. Although Daddy can't really bake, he is an amazing cook. His first few jobs when he emigrated from Greece were in restaurants. He was very helpful when we started the shop, giving us advice on how to hire a manager and the importance of good employees. In fact, he suggested we hire some employees to help us before we opened. We told him we didn't need the help as this would be a quiet little bakery, but we definitely should have listened to him!

Our dad never lost those chef skills from working in restaurants, and he did a lot of cooking at home, especially anytime meat was involved. While our grandmother taught us to bake, we learned quite a bit about cooking from our father: the use of spices, how salt enhances the flavor of food, how to sauté, how to roast, picking a good piece of meat at the butcher shop—even the right way to carve a turkey. He, like our grandmother, took pride in what he prepared. He loved having family over and cooking for everyone—especially backyard barbecues in the summer. We loved all the grilled meat he prepared during our picnics, but of course, we couldn't wait for dessert!

Our father's favorite sweet treat was coconut cream pie, and we would always make one to eat at the picnic every summer. The fresh taste of coconut and the graham-cracker crust with the creamy filling was so delicious. It's no surprise that our coconut cupcake is our father's favorite, and the one we bring him for Father's Day.

> *Our father's favorite sweet treat was coconut cream pie, and we would always make one to eat at the picnic every summer.*

Coconut Cupcakes

Makes 12 cupcakes

FOR THE CUPCAKES

2 ½ cups all-purpose flour

2 ½ teaspoons baking powder

¼ teaspoon salt

8 tablespoons unsalted butter, at room temperature (European style recommended)

1 ¾ cups sugar

2 large eggs, at room temperature

2 ¼ teaspoons pure vanilla extract (Madagascar Bourbon recommended)

1 ¼ cups whole milk, at room temperature

1 cup shredded sweetened coconut

FOR THE COCONUT CREAM-CHEESE FROSTING

4 tablespoons unsalted butter, at room temperature

6 ounces cream cheese, at room temperature

¼ teaspoon pure vanilla extract

4 cups confectioners' sugar, sifted

4 cups shredded sweetened coconut

For the cupcakes:

❶ Preheat the oven to 350°F. Line a standard cupcake pan with twelve paper baking cups, or grease the pan with butter if not using baking cups.

❷ Sift together the flour, baking powder, and salt on a sheet of parchment paper or wax paper and set aside.

❸ In the bowl of a stand mixer or in a bowl with a handheld electric mixer, cream together the butter and sugar for 3 to 5 minutes, or until light and fluffy. Add the eggs one at a time, mixing slowly after each addition.

❹ Add the vanilla to the milk in a large liquid measuring cup.

5 Add one third of the dry ingredients followed by one third of the milk, and mix thoroughly. Repeat. Stop to scrape down the bowl as needed. Add the last third of dry ingredients followed by the last third of milk. Mix thoroughly. Using a spatula, gently fold in the shredded coconut.

6 Scoop the batter into the cupcake pan using a standard-size ice-cream scoop until each cup is two-thirds full and bake for 16 to 18 minutes (start checking at 15 minutes), or until a toothpick comes out clean. Transfer the pan to a wire rack to cool completely.

For the frosting:

1 Combine the butter, cream cheese, vanilla, and confectioners' sugar in a mixer and whip together at high speed until light and airy, approximately 3 to 5 minutes.

2 Using a small offset spatula, apply a dollop (approximately 4 tablespoons) of vanilla cream-cheese frosting on top of the cupcake and spread to the edges of the cupcake so that it is completely covered with frosting. Then sprinkle shredded coconut on top of the frosting so that it forms a "cloud" of coconut on top of the cupcake. Pat down and cover the frosting with shredded coconut.

Recipe for Success

You Can't Rush a Good Thing!

It's always tempting to rush and cut corners to meet a deadline. But we've found that this just leads to more work than if the job had been done properly to begin with. Whenever we rush to bake a recipe, inevitably, something will go wrong—our project will crumble, an ingredient will be forgotten, or we'll taste a cupcake, forgetting that we need it for an order. Our advice is this: no matter the pressure, no matter what the clock says, don't scramble to get it done. Take a deep breath, focus, and be precise and careful. Also, be prepared: Make a list of ingredients or steps before you start. Draw up a sketch or a schedule. Have a backup plan in case something goes wrong (in our case, a few extra cupcakes and tons of icing for patch jobs!). Think through what you are trying to accomplish, do your best, and leave yourself enough time to do it right. We seem to always be breathlessly completing a project, but it's a surefire recipe for disaster when you consistently work this way (although it does make for some entertaining TV moments!).

Here Comes the Bride . . .

We do tons of weddings every weekend—sometimes six or seven per weekend day. And many people have proposed in our shop. That is why we are so excited that in 2010, Katherine got engaged!

Obviously, Mommy was over the moon at the news—she'd been begging Katherine to settle down for years. Katherine tells the story best:

Ben and I have been together for more than seven years, but have been dating long-distance for six of them. We met in DC at a happy hour. I was working for the Carnegie Endowment for International Peace, and he was working for the Pan-American Health Organization. As usual, life took us in different directions: he went off to law school in Chicago, and I stayed in DC. We always kept in touch, and one of us would usually fly out every other weekend to see the other . . . and I'm terrified of flying, so you can only imagine how much I liked him!

The really strange/cool thing is that my grandparents' names are also Katherine and Ben. And both of our mothers' names are Elaine! He has one older brother that is the same age as Sophie. There are a lot of similarities between our families.

Ben was finally able to transfer within his law firm (Latham & Watkins) from LA to DC in May 2010, and he proposed to me in Naples, Florida. Sophie and I had gotten into a fight the day before we were supposed to fly to see his family in Naples (they are from Denver, but were spending the weekend in Naples). I was so glad to be away from Sophie and was excited about getting a chance to go someplace sunny (which we never do, because we are always working). Ben had rented a large pontoon boat to take us out to see some dolphins and manatees. But instead, a tiny motorboat pulled up on the shore, and I refused to get in. The water was very choppy that day, and I am terrified of open water. Ben tried to coax me in, but I was not budging. Eventually I gave in even though I was scared to death, so if he was nervous about proposing, there was no way I noticed. I was too busy with my own worries!

Eventually, we got to calmer water and saw the dolphins and manatees. It was very serene. We stopped at a small private island with no one else in sight (we later found out it was a nude beach!), and that is where Ben proposed, while we were walking on the sand. I was so excited! The captain of our boat brought out a bottle of Moët & Chandon Rosé, and I was so surprised that the captain knew my favorite kind of champagne. Ben later broke it to me that he had bought the champagne, not the captain (duh!). Once we got back on the boat, he asked me if I wanted to call Sophie or my mom. I said no. I wanted to keep this just between us for the time being.

We were going to meet his parents for lunch and break the news to them then. As I walked through the doors of the restaurant I was stunned to see Sophie, my mom, my dad, my brother-in-law, and Ben's entire family there! Ben had arranged for everyone to fly down to be there for when he proposed. Everyone was in on it but me . . . so much for me keeping it a secret!

The thing that I love most about Ben is that he knows me so well. He knows how close I am to my family and how much they mean to me. He knows that even though I said I wanted to keep this a secret from them, it really wouldn't be a celebration unless they were all there. As for Sophie . . . I forgave her. Don't I always?

Once we got back to DC, it was a complete whirlwind of activity. Mommy had already announced my engagement to everyone—including random customers—before I even got through the door. Sophie ended up planning a surprise engagement party for me and making a giant engagement ring out of cupcakes. Once again, they pulled one over on me: I had thought it was a really strange week with my mother telling me she had "dental problems" she needed to tend to and Sophie going MIA. They were really planning this sweet party for me, and I was very touched.

Sophie making purple fondant for Katherine's cupcake engagement ring

Vanilla Buttercream Wedding Cupcakes

The most classic cupcake we do for weddings is our vanilla cupcake with vanilla buttercream frosting—often with the couple's initials pressed into fondant. We decorate the cupcakes with edible dragées or pearls, and they look absolutely gorgeous stacked up in a tall pyramid. To us, this beats any wedding cake!

Makes 12 cupcakes

FOR THE CUPCAKES

2 ½ cups all-purpose flour

2 ½ teaspoons baking powder

¼ teaspoon salt

8 tablespoons unsalted butter, at room temperature

1 ¾ cups sugar

2 large eggs, at room temperature

2 ¼ teaspoons pure vanilla extract

seeds from 1 vanilla bean

1 ¼ cups whole milk, at room temperature

FOR THE VANILLA BUTTERCREAM FROSTING

16 tablespoons unsalted butter, at room temperature

4 cups confectioners' sugar, sifted

1 teaspoon whole milk

1 teaspoon pure vanilla extract

⅛ teaspoon salt

FOR THE DECORATION

fondant

rubber alphabet stamps

circular or heart-shaped cookie cutter

For the cupcakes:

1 Preheat the oven to 350°F. Line a standard cupcake pan with twelve paper baking cups, or grease the pan with butter if not using baking cups.

2 Sift together the flour, baking powder, and salt on a sheet of parchment paper or wax paper and set aside.

3 In the bowl of a stand mixer or in a bowl with a handheld electric mixer, cream together the butter and sugar for 3 to 5 minutes, or until light and fluffy. Add the eggs one at a time, mixing slowly after each addition.

4 Add the vanilla extract and vanilla bean seeds to the milk in a large liquid measuring cup.

5 Add one third of the dry ingredients followed by one third of the milk, and mix thoroughly. Repeat. Stop to scrape down the bowl as needed. Add the last third of dry ingredients followed by the last third of milk. Mix slowly until fully incorporated.

6 Scoop the batter into the cupcake pan using a standard-size ice-cream scoop until the cups are two-thirds full, and bake for 16 to 18 minutes (start checking at 15 minutes) or until a toothpick comes out clean. Transfer the pan to a wire rack to cool completely.

For the frosting:

Combine the ingredients in a mixer and whip together at high speed until light and airy, approximately 3 to 5 minutes. Load the frosting into a large piping bag fitted with a large round tip and frost each cupcake with a signature swirl (see page 23).

For the decoration:

Roll out the fondant in your desired wedding (or party) colors, and using rubber alphabet stamps, stamp the desired initials into the fondant. Using a cookie cutter, cut the letters out of the fondant in a circle or heart shape and place on top of each cupcake.

Stars and Stripes

I remember my thirteenth birthday like it was yesterday. It was my favorite birthday party ever—a spa spectacular! Mommy let me invite a ton of friends from school and we were *so* excited! We had lots of vanilla cake, chocolate cupcakes, and strawberry ice cream, and stayed up all night long doing one another's hair and nails while listening to New Kids on the Block on the boom box. Katherine even invited her friends, so altogether, we took over the entire upstairs of our house!

My birthdays were always quite the celebration—even if we didn't have fireworks (Canada celebrates its independence on July 1, but I could never quite convince my parents to shoot them off for the tenth of July). Most of my birthday parties had an outdoor barbecue with hamburgers and hot dogs, summer salads, and treats. We would race around the yard, playing badminton and cops and robbers. And the cupcakes! We loved to take strawberries and raspberries from the patches in Papou's garden and throw them into our vanilla cupcake recipe. We would top cupcakes with a simple vanilla buttercream frosting and cover them in fresh raspberries and blueberries. Everyone loved them and they were gobbled up in minutes. In a word: *heaven!* I used to think I was very lucky to have my birthday in the summer, when the berries were sweetest, the nights were warmest, and the fun lingered on and on. —Sophie

July Fourth "Triple Berry" Cupcakes

We always bake a red, white, and blue cupcake for Independence Day. We love throwing raspberries, strawberries, and blueberries into our vanilla batter to give this cupcake a patriotic feel!

Makes 12 cupcakes

FOR THE CUPCAKES
2 ½ cups all-purpose flour
2 ½ teaspoons baking powder
¼ teaspoon salt
8 tablespoons unsalted butter, at room temperature
1 ¾ cups sugar
2 large eggs, at room temperature
2 ¼ teaspoons pure vanilla extract
1 ¼ cups whole milk, at room temperature
¼ cup fresh strawberries, diced

¼ cup fresh raspberries
¼ cup fresh blueberries

FOR THE VANILLA BUTTERCREAM FROSTING
See recipe, page 133.

FOR SERVING
12 mini sparklers
strawberries
raspberries
blueberries

For the cupcakes:

1 Preheat the oven to 350°F. Line a standard cupcake pan with twelve paper baking cups, or grease the pan with butter if not using baking cups.

2 Sift together the flour, baking powder, and salt on a sheet of parchment paper or wax paper and set aside.

3 In the bowl of a stand mixer or in a bowl with a handheld electric mixer, cream together the butter and sugar for 3 to 5 minutes, or until light and fluffy. Add the eggs one at a time, mixing slowly after each addition.

4 Add the vanilla to the milk in a large liquid measuring cup.

⑤ Add one third of the dry ingredients followed by one third of the milk, and mix thoroughly. Repeat. Stop to scrape down the bowl as needed. Add the last third of the dry ingredients followed by the last third of the milk. Mix slowly until well incorporated. Using a spatula, gently fold in the berries.

⑥ Scoop the batter into a cupcake pan using a standard-size ice-cream scoop until the cups are two-thirds full, and bake for 16 to 18 minutes (start checking at 15 minutes), or until a toothpick comes out clean. Transfer the pan to a wire rack to cool completely.

For the frosting:

See recipe, page 133. Load the frosting into a piping bag fitted with a large round tip and frost each cupcake with a signature swirl (see page 23).

For serving:

To garnish the cupcakes with a patriotic theme, cover them with strawberries, raspberries, and blueberries, then top with a sparkler and serve!

DECEMBER 2010

Operation Cupcake

Katherine and I love living in the United States, especially in Washington, DC. We are really proud of owning a small business in Washington and being able to create jobs for people in our bakery—this really is the American dream! I became a citizen after living here for thirteen years. I remember going in to take my citizenship test and I passed on the spot. Then, to my surprise, I was told my citizenship ceremony was in one hour! I had no idea that I was going to be sworn in the same day I took my test. I would have dressed better! All the people around me, from all these different countries, were dressed in their Sunday best. I, instead, was wearing a tank top, cargo crop pants, and flip-flops to my swearing-in ceremony! I was mortified, but I was very proud to get my citizenship certificate and am proud to be a dual citizen of both Canada and the United States.

Katherine and I have many family and friends in the armed forces who served in Iraq and Afghanistan. We have always wanted to do something for the troops overseas—but we just didn't know how or who to contact. Then one day, we got a call from the Pentagon. We were in shock—the chairman of the Joint Chiefs of Staff (he reports directly to the president!) reached out to us for some baking lessons for the Pentagon chefs. We said we'd love to help and that we also wanted to donate ten thousand cupcakes to the troops overseas. It was a once-in-a-lifetime opportunity for us—so monumental, we could hardly believe it. We immediately had our head baker, Andres, order all the supplies we needed: 500 pounds of sugar, 50 gallons of milk, 100 dozen eggs, 500 pounds of flour, 200 pounds of butter, 1,500 pounds of confectioners' sugar, 300 pounds of cream cheese, and 100 extra cupcake pans! It was like squishing two days' worth of baking cupcakes into one, and we were sweating. But there was no looking back: "Operation Cupcake" was under way!

We took Mommy and two of our employees with us, packed our supplies in a huge truck, and met up with the five chefs we would be baking with. They told us they had a surprise for us: we were going to have a little contest to see what cupcake would go to the troops. We had a bake-off with five flavors, and they chose carrot cupcakes (we ended up sending half carrot, and the other half an assortment since we just knew some people would love chocolate cupcakes).

This was the most meaningful thing we've ever done in our lives. We watched from the tarmac as our cupcakes were loaded onto a military plane. A few days later, the Pentagon sent us footage of the army bringing 108 boxes to the base at Islamabad, Pakistan. One of the soldiers said, "Thanks, it's nice to have a little piece of home here."

Top: Soldiers unload boxes of cupcakes at Forward Operating Base Zerok, one of the more remote and dangerous Forward Operating Bases in Afghanistan. *Bottom:* The 10,000 cupcakes were transported aboard a C-17 on a pallet and kept cool with dry ice for the long air trip to the troops in Iraq and Afghanistan. The cupcakes arrived in perfect condition.

It was something so small for us to make these cupcakes, but it meant a huge amount to these brave men and women. It's our way of saying thank you for all they do. Mission accomplished! —Sophie

Recipe for Success

Lead by Example

The military may be the best organization in the world at instilling leadership qualities. But even if you're not in the armed forces, it doesn't mean you can't be a great leader. The best leaders don't just bellow orders; they lead by example. They act the way they expect their followers to act. They convey the importance of paying attention to details, treating people with respect, setting reasonable deadlines and expectations, striving for perfection, and seeing a task through to completion. And what works in the workplace also works in the home: good parents are role models as well, and this prevents children from developing bad habits and instills in them a strong work ethic, compassion, and confidence. Our parents raised us this way, through showing, not just telling. We're better people—and better businesswomen—because of it.

Carrot Cupcakes

Makes 18 cupcakes

FOR THE CUPCAKES
2 ½ cups all-purpose flour
3 teaspoons baking powder
1 teaspoon ground cinnamon
½ teaspoon salt
16 tablespoons unsalted butter, at room
    temperature
2 cups sugar
4 large eggs, at room temperature

⅓ cup hot water
2 cups freshly grated carrots
½ cup freshly grated apple (approximately
    1 medium-size apple—we use Gala apples,
    but you can use your favorite type)

FOR THE VANILLA CREAM-CHEESE FROSTING
See recipe, page 20.

For the cupcakes:

1 Preheat the oven to 350°F. Line a standard cupcake pan with twelve paper baking cups, and a second pan with six baking cups, or grease pans with butter if not using baking cups.

2 Sift together the flour, baking powder, cinnamon, and salt on a sheet of parchment paper or wax paper and set aside.

3 Place the butter in the bowl of a stand mixer or in a bowl with a handheld electric mixer. Beat on medium speed until fluffy. Stop to add the sugar; beat on medium speed until well incorporated.

4 Add the eggs one at a time, mixing slowly after each addition.

5 Reduce the speed to low. At this stage, it's always important to mix as slowly and as little as necessary since you don't want to traumatize your batter.

6 Add one third of the flour mixture to the butter mixture, then gradually add one third of the hot water, beating until well incorporated. Add another third of the flour mixture, followed by one third of the hot water. Stop to scrape down the bowl as needed. Add the remaining flour mixture, followed by the remaining hot water, and beat just until combined.

7 Using a spatula, fold the grated carrot and apple into the batter.

8 Use a standard-size ice-cream scoop to fill each baking cup with batter, so that the wells are two-thirds full. Bake for 18 to 20 minutes (start checking at 15 minutes), or until a toothpick inserted into the center of a cupcake comes out clean. Transfer the pan to a wire rack to cool completely.

For the vanilla cream-cheese frosting:

See recipe, page 20. Then you can decorate with little fondant carrots if you like!

One frosting, ten flavors!

With only one ingredient in addition to our basic cream-cheese frosting, you can make ten different types of icing for your cupcakes! It's super easy and super fun!

Chocolate Frosting—add ½ cup melted (and cooled) semisweet chocolate chips

Peanut Butter Frosting—add ¼ cup creamy peanut butter

Lemon Frosting—add the juice and zest of 2 lemons

Maple Frosting—add ¼ cup maple syrup

Lime Frosting—add the juice and zest of 3 limes

Cinnamon Frosting—add 2 teaspoons ground cinnamon

Orange Frosting—add the juice and zest of 1 orange

Cookies & Crème Frosting—add ¼ cup crushed Oreo cookies

Mocha Frosting—add ¼ cup cold coffee

Toffee Frosting—add ¼ cup crushed toffee candy

Lemonade-Stand Days

AUGUST 1982

Starting a business is a risky endeavor—this we know firsthand. But we're not just talking about our decision to open Georgetown Cupcake. Our first venture together was actually when we were five and four years old. We opened a lemonade stand in our grandparents' driveway. Things were a little different back then. It didn't matter how much lemonade we sold or what hours we worked. We didn't even have to pay our landlords rent! Yet our sales philosophy was pretty much the same as it is today: just put out a great product and people will love it.

Neighbors would stop by and pay twenty-five cents for a cup of refreshing lemonade. It was the quality of product we were most concerned with. Babee would cut the lemons into halves and we would squeeze them using her glass orange juicer. We added a few scoops of sugar and our secret ingredient, the zest of some of the lemon. It was the zest that really gave it that zing! In the afternoon, we would carry out all our plastic cups and pitchers of lemonade and sit on our lawn chairs at the end of the driveway, waiting for people to pass by. We would sit and talk and have a glass ourselves. And at the end of the day, we counted up our earnings and split it: a whole four dollars. That could buy a lot of bags of chips at the corner store!

Our Lemon Blossom cupcake was inspired by those days making fresh-squeezed lemonade together. Sometimes we even throw the Lemon Blossom cupcakes in the freezer. On a humid day it is so refreshing to bite into that cold, tangy lemon frosting and cake, almost like sinking your teeth into an ice-cream cupcake. *Ahhhh.*

Lemon Blossom Cupcakes

Makes 12 cupcakes

FOR THE CUPCAKES

2 ½ cups all-purpose flour

2 ½ teaspoons baking powder

¼ teaspoon salt

8 tablespoons unsalted butter, at room
  temperature

1 ¾ cups sugar

2 large eggs, at room temperature

2 ¼ teaspoons pure vanilla extract

1 ¼ cups whole milk, at room temperature

½ cup freshly squeezed lemon juice

½ cup freshly grated lemon zest (2 to 3
  lemons)

FOR THE LEMON CREAM-CHEESE FROSTING

4 tablespoons unsalted butter, at room
  temperature

6 ounces cream cheese, at room temperature

4 cups confectioners' sugar, sifted

½ teaspoon pure vanilla extract

½ cup freshly grated lemon zest (2 to 3
  lemons)

For the cupcakes:

❶ Preheat the oven to 350°F. Line a standard cupcake pan with twelve paper baking cups, or grease the pan with butter if not using baking cups.

❷ Sift together the flour, baking powder, and salt on a sheet of parchment paper or wax paper and set aside.

❸ In the bowl of a stand mixer or in a bowl with a handheld electric mixer, cream together the butter and sugar for 3 to 5 minutes, or until light and fluffy. Add the eggs one at a time, mixing slowly after each addition.

❹ Add the vanilla to the milk in a large liquid measuring cup.

5 Add one third of the dry ingredients followed by one third of the milk, and mix thoroughly. Repeat. Stop to scrape down the bowl as needed. Add the last third of dry ingredients followed by the last third of milk. Mix slowly until just incorporated. Add lemon juice and zest, and mix thoroughly at low speed.

6 Scoop the batter into the cupcake pan using a standard-size ice-cream scoop until the cups are two-thirds full, and bake for 16 to 18 minutes (start checking at 15 minutes), or until a toothpick comes out clean. Transfer the pan to a wire rack to cool completely.

sisters' baking secret
add some zip with zest

Lemon zest adds a little kick to a recipe. Using a fine grater or a zester, rub the lemon in one direction against the blades. Turn the lemon as you go, so you only remove the yellow skin; the white part underneath is bitter. If the strands of skin are long and thin, you can use a knife to chop them finer. This way, they'll blend better into the mixture of whatever you are baking. ✱

For the frosting:

Combine the ingredients in a mixer and whip together at high speed until light and airy, approximately 3 to 5 minutes. Frost the cupcakes with the signature swirl (see page 23), and top with a lemon wedge or piece of lemon zest!

Recipe for Success

Patience Is a Virtue, in Baking and in Business

*W*e've always been a little anxious: we had a hard time waiting for Babee's cupcakes and cakes to cool so we could frost them. But she taught us that if you don't wait, the frosting will melt and slide off in a messy heap. So we sat on our hands, asking every five minutes if it was time yet. Though agonizing, it taught us patience.

In business, it's very tempting to race ahead with your plans too soon. You want to be profitable; you want your business to boom. But it's better to take your time to perfect your product before you expand—we didn't start off with all eighty flavors that first month, and we certainly took our time to grow our shop and our staff. Part of being successful is knowing when your ideas are fully baked and ready to be improved upon. And if your business isn't a success right off the bat, be patient as well. Most people don't have a line around the block the first day (we were very lucky!). It takes time to get the word out, time for people to learn about you and appreciate what you have to offer.

Babee's Baklava   Our father's family still lives in Greece, so every other summer we would go to Greece and visit with them. We love visiting Greece—especially the small villages where our parents are from, because we find it peaceful and calming. There is something about escaping to a place where there are cute lambs and sheep strolling across the mountain roads, chickens running carelessly all over, and cows mooing in the background. When we wake up to the sound of the rooster's *cock-a-doodle-doo* in the morning, we *know* we aren't in Washington anymore! Sure, there are a lot of creature comforts we have to do without—no air conditioning (which is brutal) and sometimes no hot water (yikes!)—but we always enjoy our visits to Greece.

In August 2006, one of our cousins was getting married, so our whole family flew over for the wedding. Weddings are a big village affair and usually take place in the summer months so everyone can celebrate in the streets. The party started the night before the wedding, with dancing to a live Greek band and feasting on Greek foods and desserts, including our favorite, baklava. By the end of the three-day celebration, we were stuffed and blissfully exhausted.

Makes about 24 servings

3 cups ground walnuts

½ cup sugar

1 teaspoon ground cinnamon

1 package phyllo dough (Babee made her own from scratch, but because it is so thin and fragile, it's easier just to buy it at the supermarket. The phyllo comes in sheets. Once the package is opened, keep the sheets from drying out by placing a clean damp dish cloth over them.)

16 tablespoons unsalted butter, melted

SYRUP

1 cup sugar

1 cup clover honey

1 cup water

1 large orange, sliced

½ cup brandy (optional)

1 cinnamon stick

1 Preheat the oven to 350°F.

2 Mix together walnuts, sugar, and cinnamon.

3 Butter a large square baking pan by applying the melted butter with a pastry brush. Lay down one sheet of phyllo dough. Butter the dough with the pastry brush. Repeat five times so you have six layers of buttered phyllo.

4 Then, add ⅓ cup of the walnut mixture, sprinkling it across the sheet of phyllo in an even layer.

5 Add another sheet of phyllo, and butter it. Add ⅓ cup of the walnut mixture. Repeat until all the walnut mixture is used up.

6 Add six more sheets of phyllo on top, buttering each sheet.

7 Using a sharp knife, cut the baklava into diamond shapes. Bake for 40 minutes, or until golden brown.

For the syrup:

Put all the ingredients in a large saucepan and boil on medium-high heat for 5 minutes. Let cool. Remove the orange slices and cinnamon stick and pour on top of the baklava as soon as it comes out of the oven.

Left: Sophie and Katherine with their great aunt Constance, Greece 2006
Bottom: Katherine, Sophie, and cousin Lena, Greece 1985

Part 5

BEHIND THE
SCENES

*Fun behind-the-scenes stories and
recipes from seasons one
and two of DC Cupcakes*

13. ⊚ DC CUPCAKES

....

"I'm Sophie . . . and I'm Katherine. We're sisters and business partners. We ditched our corporate jobs to follow our dreams, to work together and make the world's best tasting cupcakes. It's not going to be easy. . . ." So starts every episode of *DC Cupcakes* on TLC. We've finished two seasons and have more episodes on the way—which is crazy! We never thought we'd have our own bakery, much less our own TV show. We feel so lucky, especially for the fans who make the trip to our bakery in DC from far away or who stop us on the street to tell us how much they love the show.

Filming *DC Cupcakes* is a ton of fun. When we're in production, we have cameras following us around in the bakery every day—usually two of them from 7:00 A.M. to 8:00 P.M.! Sometimes when we are pulling an all-nighter, the camera crews will set up a time-lapse camera to watch us. At first we were intimidated with cameras following our every move. We were nervous and embarrassed about screwing things up on camera and worried about what our hair and makeup looked like. Well, that quickly went out the window! While we're working, we honestly do forget that the cameras are there because we are so focused on getting our projects and work finished. By the end of most episodes, our hair and makeup are a disaster—but that's how it is in real life! You don't have time to stop and fix your lip gloss when you are in the middle of frosting ten thousand cupcakes and going at lightning speed all day! The camera crew became family; we spent every day, all day, with them, and they witnessed our ups and downs, our emotional highs and lows. They were there through it all.

Choosing which orders and projects to feature on *DC Cupcakes* is always a difficult task. We have so many fun orders in our catering binder and we can't feature them all, so we go through our binder and choose a variety of projects that represent different cupcake techniques. We also try to spread them out so we don't run ourselves too ragged!

Everyone loves to comment on our *DC Cupcakes* uniforms—our trademark pink aprons and pink wellies! The truth is we love wearing wellies in our bakery because we have ruined so many pairs of shoes spilling ingredients on them. When you are working in a bakery, there is always flour spilling, sugar falling, and batter dripping everywhere, and there is nothing worse than Red Velvet batter on a brand-new pair of leather shoes. So, we switched to wellies and at the end of the day, we just hose our boots down so they are good as new! We love the color pink, so naturally, our wellies and aprons are pink, just like our boxes.

Here is the inside scoop on all of our episodes (including some stuff that never made it on air!) and recipes for the featured cupcakes.

Episode: "Mardi Gras"

Our very first episode! It was Valentine's Day 2010, and we baked and sold 25,000 cupcakes in 14 different flavors—a new record for Georgetown Cupcake. During the episode, the flour was flying; Katherine even wound up covered in cocoa, trying to mix up another batch of 150 dozen Red Velvets! The line was down the block and people were waiting up to an hour for one of our cupcakes. So of course, we wanted to make everyone happy, and were working like crazy to keep up with the demand. When we finally closed the shop at 9:00 P.M., we heaved a sigh of relief. But then it was back to work, since Sophie promised St. Jude's we'd make 1,000 minis in the shape of a Mardi Gras mask as a centerpiece for their fund-raiser. How could we say no to those kids?

So off to the lab we went, sculpting a huge mask out of cereal treats, frosting it in berry-colored buttercream, and attaching purple and gold cupcakes. We left at 4:30 A.M., utterly exhausted. But when we came back in the morning . . . disaster! The mask had fallen apart, and the cupcakes were ruined. It was back to the drawing board and a mad scramble to get the mask rebuilt and the cupcakes rebaked in time for the event. We pitched in as a team and made it—with thirty minutes to spare. But then we couldn't get the massive display out the door of the lab! Georgetown buildings are really old, and their doors are really narrow. Luckily, one of our staff had a quick fix: she took a hammer to the door hinges and ripped off the door, so we could squeeze the cupcake mask—without an inch to spare—through the door frame. We raced to the St. Jude's party and set up the display. As we stood there, catching our breath, we were amazed to hear a bidding war going on over the baking lessons we had donated to the auction. We raised $1,600 for the charity and were so proud. It was a crazy day, but typical of what goes on at Georgetown Cupcake, and a great way to introduce viewers to our lives and our bakery.

What you didn't see: Sophie had a hunch the mask was going to fall—it actually started to lean around 3:00 A.M. She wanted to stay and babysit it, but Mommy was so tired and convinced us all to go home, get a few hours' sleep, and shower. If we had stayed, the mask might have been saved!

Berry-Infused Purple Buttercream Frosting

16 tablespoons unsalted butter, at room
   temperature
4 cups confectioners' sugar, sifted
1 teaspoon whole milk
1 teaspoon pure vanilla extract
⅛ teaspoon salt

¼ cup blueberry juice (squeezed from fresh
   blueberries)
¼ cup strawberry juice (squeezed from fresh
   strawberries)
red or blue gel food color (if desired)

Combine the butter, confectioners' sugar, milk, vanilla, and salt in the bowl of a stand mixer or in a bowl with a handheld electric mixer and mix at high speed for 3 to 5 minutes, or until light and airy. Slowly add the blueberry and strawberry juice, mixing at low speed. It's important to be patient! Mix on high speed for an additional 4 to 5 minutes, until juice is completely absorbed. If food color is desired, add a tiny amount (⅛ teaspoon) of no-taste red or blue gel food color. Mix on high speed for an additional 2 to 3 minutes.

Episode: "Pupcakes"

When we got older and moved out of our childhood home, Mommy replaced us with Poochie, her naughty but loveable Siberian Husky. (Sophie thinks Poochie looks a little like Katherine!) One day at the dog park with Poochie, we met with Dr. Gary from the Washington Animal Rescue League to discuss his fund-raising gala and how we could help. The league does great things; they have about two hundred dogs, all available for adoption—and we *love* dogs. We offered to create a centerpiece for the party: a giant life-size dog made out of cupcakes that would serve five hundred people! We also wanted to bake special "doggy" cupcakes to feed the pooches and sell special cupcakes at the shop to benefit the league.

Since the shop was growing, we realized we needed to teach more people to do our signature swirl. Sophie is a control freak—she doesn't trust people to do our swirl. Frosting is really an artistic part of the process—and it's not as easy as it looks. But we needed help, or we would be stuck frosting cupcakes forever. So we had a little competition: we called in three employees to test their skills. The first was a little too wild.

The second couldn't hold the piping bag closed, and the frosting came out the top. The third was a natural: she got it right the first time and we put her straight to work so we could hit the lab and start our doggie project!

We each came up with our own "pupcake" recipes and decided we would let Poochie be the judge. Sophie made a modified version of our banana chocolate-chip cupcake with honey, applesauce, rolled oats, carob chips, and a peanut butter frosting, while Katherine did chicken and sweet potato, which smelled a little like chicken soup. Poochie knocked over Katherine's bowl—and he wouldn't even eat it off the floor. Sophie won!

For the gala centerpiece, we decided to make a giant Dalmatian, sculpted out of chicken wire with foam inside. We thought it was looking great, but Andres laughed at us. Hey, we're cupcake bakers, not sculptors! He suggested we get some professional help, and we couldn't agree more. So we enlisted a friend of ours, an artist, to save the day. His dog was amazing! We stuffed him with newspaper and nontoxic foam so we could attach the cupcakes to the dog. We used coconut cupcakes to make him look furry (Mommy thought he looked more like a sheepdog than a Dalmatian). Our fondant artist did fondant for the eyes, nose, ears, and tail, and fondant butterflies and lady bugs to put on our "grass" cupcakes. When we loaded the cupcake dog in the car, Poochie jumped in right after it and almost knocked it over. He thought it was his girlfriend!

At the event, everyone loved our centerpiece—even though he lost his nose on the way in and we had to do a quick buttercream glue job on site. And the dogs went wild for our pupcakes. We also felt great that sales of the benefit cupcakes in our shop raised two thousand dollars for the league. We told Dr. Gary to count us in every year to cater cupcakes for this fabulous event.

What you didn't see: Poochie ran away between scenes! When we were making the pupcakes in the lab, somebody left the door open and Poochie bolted and ran down

M Street. One of our camera guys chased him for about a mile and finally caught him. We were all scared, running down M Street in our pink aprons screaming, "Poochie!"

Sophie's Pupcakes

Makes 12 pupcakes

FOR THE PUPCAKES

2 large eggs

1 cup applesauce, unsweetened

3 teaspoons ground cinnamon

1 cup rolled oats

½ cup carob chips

3 bananas, mashed

1 cup whole-wheat flour, sifted

½ cup creamy (smooth) peanut butter, melted

1 tablespoon honey

FOR THE FROSTING

1 cup carob chips, melted

1 cup creamy (smooth) peanut butter, melted

For the pupcakes:

❶ Preheat the oven to 350°F. Line a standard cupcake pan with twelve paper baking cups, or grease the pan with butter if not using baking cups.

❷ Mix all ingredients in the bowl of a stand mixer or in a bowl with a handheld electric mixer.

❸ Using a standard-size ice-cream scoop, scoop the batter into the cupcake pan and bake for 20 to 22 minutes (start checking at 15 minutes). Transfer the pan to a wire rack to cool completely.

❹ When the pupcakes have cooled, remove them from their paper baking cups, if desired. You can leave the paper baking cups on for serving as long as you make sure your dog doesn't eat them!

For the frosting:

1 While the pupcakes are baking, melt the carob chips in the microwave for approximately 1 minute. Then melt the peanut butter in the microwave, also for about 1 minute.

2 Dip the pupcakes into the melted carob chips, and then using a fork, drizzle the melted peanut butter on top of the carob coating.

3 Serve to your dogs!

Note: This recipe is also safe for humans.

Episode: "Roller Girls"

We decided it was time to come up with a new flavor. During the first two years, we created sixty-two original flavors for Georgetown Cupcake, from Cherry Blossom to Salted Caramel. What could we do now that would wow our customers? We thought maybe something seasonal, for the warmer weather, was the way to go. We decided to call another one of our friends, a gourmet food importer. He has the best spices. He was one of the first people we met when setting up our bakery, and he believed in us from the very beginning. He showed us colored sugars in gorgeous flavors like violet, rose, and lavender. For our new flavor, we asked him for something insane—something no one would ever put in a cupcake, and he took us to the back of his storage space. He poured us a shot of hibiscus syrup. It's sweet and smells like a hibiscus flower. We took a case and raced back to the shop to start experimenting. We made a vanilla cake and mixed up three separate batches with mango, peach, and rum along with the syrup. You can be as scientific as you want coming up with new recipes, but in the end, it's a lot of guesswork. When we sampled them, the Hibiscus Mango was the definite winner—it was amazing. We decorated the cupcakes with painted fondant flowers and sprinkled them with flavored sugars. They made our entire window display look like springtime—which was very welcome after the rough winter we had in DC.

Meanwhile, we had our next big project to start: a massive six-by-six-foot DC Roller Girls logo made from a thousand cupcakes to be displayed at half-time, plus thirteen hundred more cupcakes to hand out to the team's fans. Mommy kept interrupting us—which made it very hard to create the cupcake grid. We were supposed to be there at one, and by one-thirty we still had a hundred cupcakes left to frost. The Roller Girls were calling, asking where we were and why the cupcakes weren't there yet. We were so stressed! We finally got there and had only an hour to set up. We could hear the crowds cheering and the roller girls going around—and we could barely concentrate. In the end, it turned out fine. The Roller Girls helped us hand out the cupcakes to the crowd and everyone was happy. All the stress we went through was completely forgotten when we saw everyone so excited with the cupcakes. Phew!

What you didn't see: Our "reconstructive surgery" on the Roller Girl's face! We were rushing so much to get the portrait put together in time that we didn't turn the cupcakes carefully enough to match them up. When we stepped back to take a look, it didn't look like the logo, just a mess of colors. We had to do some major repairs before we rolled her out. Luckily, we brought extra cupcakes and icing with us and were able to fix it in time!

Hibiscus Mango Cupcakes

Makes 12 cupcakes

Note: If you can't find hibiscus syrup in your grocery store, you can leave it out and still make delicious mango cupcakes.

FOR THE CUPCAKES

2 ½ cups all-purpose flour

2 ½ teaspoons baking powder

¼ teaspoon salt

8 tablespoons unsalted butter, at room temperature

1 ¾ cups sugar

2 large eggs, at room temperature

2 ¼ teaspoons pure vanilla extract

1 ¼ cups whole milk, at room temperature

½ cup hibiscus syrup (available in specialty food stores)

1 cup fresh mango, diced

FOR THE HIBISCUS BUTTERCREAM FROSTING

16 tablespoons unsalted butter, at room temperature

4 cups confectioners' sugar, sifted

1 teaspoon whole milk

1 teaspoon pure vanilla extract

⅛ teaspoon salt

¼ cup hibiscus syrup

For the cupcakes:

1 Preheat the oven to 350°F. Line a standard cupcake pan with twelve paper baking cups, or grease the pan with butter if not using baking cups.

2 Sift together the flour, baking powder, and salt on a sheet of parchment paper or wax paper and set aside.

3 In the bowl of a stand mixer or in a bowl with a handheld electric mixer, cream together the butter and sugar for 3 to 5 minutes, or until light and fluffy. Add the eggs one at a time, mixing slowly after each addition.

4 Add the vanilla to the milk in a large liquid measuring cup.

5 Add one third of the dry ingredients followed by one third of the milk, and mix thoroughly. Repeat. Stop to scrape down the bowl as needed. Add the last third of the dry ingredients, followed by the last third of the milk. Mix slowly until just incorporated. Add the hibiscus syrup and mix thoroughly at low speed. Using a spatula, gently fold the diced mango into the batter.

6 Scoop the batter into a cupcake pan using a standard-size ice-cream scoop until cups are two-thirds full, and bake for 16 to 18 minutes (start checking at 15 minutes) or until a toothpick comes out clean. Transfer the pan to a wire rack to cool completely.

For the frosting:

1 Combine the ingredients in a mixer and whip together at high speed until light and airy, approximately 3 to 5 minutes.

2 Scoop the frosting into a large piping bag fitted with a large round tip and frost each cupcake with a signature swirl (see page 23). Decorate with a fresh hibiscus blossom or a fondant flower.

Episode: "Greek Festival"

Father Steve from the Greek Orthodox Church came into the shop to visit us and Mommy (he calls us Sophia and Katerina). He asked us to display flyers and posters for the St. Sophia Cathedral's annual Greek festival, and Mommy asked if we could donate some cupcakes for the festival. It was the very next day, and she put us on the spot! But she was so excited, we said we'd do it. We volunteered to make an "authentic" Greek cupcake from one of our grandmas' recipes, and decided to replicate the huge piece of ancient Greek art from the festival poster with the cupcakes. We'd frost them in chocolate and copper-colored buttercream.

Meanwhile, one of our employees at the store was having some excitement of her own. She had a crush on this cute guy in her class, and he stopped by the store. To impress him, she gave him a Red Velvet cupcake—with a heart on top. It cracked us up that she was blushing the entire time.

For the festival, we thought of making Revani—the orange-flavored Greek cake made with semolina (see recipe, page 46)—but Mommy had her own ideas. She showed up with a cluster of grapes and some sweet wine. She explained that they were used to make Greek must, a grape syrup, and that it was delicious. Mommy is not a great chef, but she is great at being Greek! So we mashed the grapes by hand, stems and all, and put the juice through a strainer, just how they do it in Greece. We used traditional Greek ingredients in the cupcake: orange juice, cinnamon, cloves, brandy, olive oil, sweet wine, and walnuts. As we baked, we yelled, *"Opa!"* Translation: "Party!"

Back at the shop, our love-struck staff member nearly caught the shop on fire. After being put in charge of stirring the ganache, she started texting her friends and forgot to keep stirring, and the bowl almost caught on fire. Good thing we were in the lab and missed it!

The Greek mural was huge: we had to build it in four pieces and use fifteen hundred mini cupcakes. And we actually finished on schedule—it must have been divine

intervention. Sometimes the hardest part of the project isn't making it, it's delivering it. So of course, we had trouble fitting the mural in our minivan. But we knew we had to get it there; this is a huge event for our family, and both Mommy and our daddy never miss it. The best part of coming to the festival is seeing all the traditional things: the food, the music, the dancing. And we were excited to add cupcakes! Taking part in the Greek festival made us think of our beloved Babee. On the display table, we placed a framed photo of Babee. She's our inspiration, and we felt she was with us on this day.

We were close to putting our Greek mural together at the festival when we dropped several cupcakes. Everyone was watching, which made us even more nervous. It was totally embarrassing. Luckily, we had brought extra cupcakes and frosting, and we were able to salvage the mural. We also brought tons of different cupcakes to sell to raise money for the church. They sold so well, there wasn't even one Greek cupcake left for Father Steve.

What you didn't see: Katherine snuck off to eat souvlaki during the bake sale, leaving Sophie alone. Sophie was so mad because Katherine didn't even bring her one back!

Greek Grape Must Cupcakes

Makes 12 cupcakes

FOR THE GRAPE MUST
5 pounds red grapes

FOR THE CUPCAKES
1 ¼ cups all-purpose flour
1 ½ teaspoons baking powder
¼ teaspoon salt
¼ teaspoon ground cinnamon
¼ teaspoon ground nutmeg
¼ teaspoon ground cloves

8 tablespoons unsalted butter,
   at room temperature
1 cup sugar
2 eggs, at room temperature
½ cup grape must syrup
1 tablespoon honey
⅓ cup water

FOR SERVING
½ cup confectioners' sugar, sifted
½ cup grape must

For the grape must:

Squeeze the grapes using your hands. Pour into a pot with the stems and grape skins, and boil on medium heat for 1 hour, until the juice thickens to a syrup. Pour the syrup through a strainer and set aside in a glass bowl. Five pounds of grapes should yield slightly more than 1 cup grape must.

For the cupcakes:

1 Preheat the oven to 350°F. Line a standard cupcake pan with twelve paper baking cups, or grease the pan with butter if not using baking cups.

2 Sift together the flour, baking powder, salt, cinnamon, and nutmeg on a piece of parchment paper or wax paper and set aside.

3 Cream together butter and sugar for 3 to 5 minutes, or until light and fluffy.

4 Add the eggs one at a time, mixing slowly after each addition.

5 Add the grape must syrup and honey, and mix slowly until well incorporated.

6 Add one third of the dry ingredients, followed by one third of the water, and mix thoroughly. Repeat. Stop to scrape down the bowl as needed. Add the last third of the dry ingredients followed by the last third of the water and mix slowly until well incorporated.

7 Using a standard-size ice-cream scoop, scoop batter into the cupcake pan until each cup is two-thirds full, and bake for 18 to 20 minutes (start checking at 15 minutes) or until a toothpick comes out clean. Transfer the pan to a wire rack to cool completely.

8 Using a fork, pierce holes in each cupcake and pour remaining grape must over the cupcakes, letting it soak in. Dust each cupcake with confectioners' sugar and serve. Enjoy!

Episode: "Wedding Recipe"

We met with a couple who wanted cupcakes instead of a cake for their wedding. The bride wanted a traditional German cake called Butter Kuchen to represent her side of the family, while the groom wanted a Filipino cake called Cassava from his family. We were very excited to start experimenting and blended the two flavors together into a batter. When we baked them, they tasted terrible—the worst flavor we've ever made. Then we came up with an idea of making a mini wedding cake consisting of two cupcakes, one larger, and one mini stacked on top of the other. Each layer would be one of the flavors. It worked—both flavors were yummy. We iced them and covered them in white fondant, decorating the mini cakes with oyster pearls and thirteen hundred edible flowers. It was simple and elegant and we loved the design. Now all we had to do was make fifty of them! It took us almost the entire night. At 3:00 A.M. we crashed, falling asleep on the floor of the lab for a mere two hours. Sometimes you have to pull an all-nighter—what can we say?

We were really worried about making it to the reception on time (what else is new?). We managed to get the cupcakes delivered, but then our driver's truck broke down, and we couldn't get the display there. We sent one of our new employees to search around the hotel for something to place the mini wedding cakes on. Could anything else go wrong? Of course! We dropped an entire box of edible flowers—almost a hundred dollars' worth—on the floor. Luckily, our employee found some black wooden boxes, and we stacked them into a makeshift display. We had thirty minutes till the bride and groom arrived, so we madly placed cakes and tea lights on the table. When we stepped back, it looked great—and the newlyweds loved it. What a relief! We definitely dodged a bullet with this one.

What you didn't see: So much for calm and cool! We were so frantic at the venue, we were crying and swearing a lot more than the cameras showed (some of those expletives just don't belong on TV). We take weddings very seriously and this was the first time something like this happened. We were a total mess putting it together on-site!

Butter Kuchen Cupcakes

This recipe is based on a traditional German Butter Kuchen recipe except that we don't use yeast. We gave it a Georgetown Cupcake twist to make it sweeter and less breadlike. Butter Kuchen traditionally does not have a frosting—instead it has a cinnamon-sugar topping!

Makes 12 cupcakes

FOR THE CUPCAKES

2 ½ cups all-purpose flour

2 ½ teaspoons baking powder

¼ teaspoon salt

2 teaspoons ground cinnamon

8 tablespoons unsalted butter, at room temperature

1 ¾ cups sugar

2 large eggs, at room temperature

2 ¼ teaspoons pure vanilla extract

1 ¼ cups whole milk, at room temperature

FOR THE CINNAMON-SUGAR TOPPING

⅓ cup ground cinnamon

⅓ cup sugar

For the cupcakes:

1 Preheat the oven to 350°F. Line a standard cupcake pan with twelve paper baking cups, or grease the pan with butter if not using baking cups.

2 Sift together the flour, baking powder, salt, and cinnamon on a sheet of parchment paper or wax paper and set aside.

3 In the bowl of a stand mixer or in a bowl with a handheld electric mixer, cream together the butter and sugar for 3 to 5 minutes, or until light and fluffy. Add the eggs one at a time, mixing slowly after each addition.

4 Add the vanilla to the milk in a large liquid measuring cup.

5 Add one third of the dry ingredients followed by one third of the milk, and mix thoroughly. Repeat. Stop to scrape down the bowl as needed. Add the last third of dry ingredients followed by the last third of milk. Mix thoroughly.

6 Scoop the batter into the cupcake pan using a standard-size ice-cream scoop until each cup is two-thirds full.

For the topping:

1 Mix together the cinnamon and sugar and spoon it evenly on top of the batter in each cupcake well.

2 Bake for 16 to 18 minutes (start checking at 15 minutes), or until a toothpick comes out clean. The cinnamon and sugar should have caramelized and be slightly crunchy to the touch. Transfer the pan to a wire rack to cool completely.

Episode: "Fire House"

The episode started off with a mom bringing us fabric swatches from her daughter's sweet-sixteen dress to create custom colors for her cupcakes. The idea was to put rose-shaped cupcakes into flowerpot centerpieces. Mommy was working with Andres on the two flavors for the cupcakes—maple and caramel. The batter is a similar color, so you usually place little caramel candies on the tray so you know which one is caramel. But when these cupcakes came out, there was no candy on the tray and we weren't sure which was which. It turned out that one of our staff had eaten the candy—Mommy was so happy she wasn't to blame this time!

When the mother came by, she was very unhappy with the color of the roses— they didn't look like the orange swatch she had provided. Since the customer is, of course, always right, we offered her a cupcake and a cup of coffee, and said we'd redo them in an hour. She watched us the entire time in the kitchen. We purposely designed our kitchen behind glass so people can see us bake, but at times like this . . . it's a major stress! She looked so angry as we remixed the frosting. But in the end, she was delighted. The cupcakes were perfect.

Firefighters are some of our regular customers, so when one came in and asked us to bake cupcakes for a fire department award ceremony the next day, we were happy to oblige. We offered to create a giant fire truck out of cupcakes . . . which was a huge order with only twenty-four hours' notice. When we get caught up in the excitement, we tend to overpromise. Our firefighter friend also asked if we would come to the firehouse and teach the guys how to bake—and we turned it into a bake-off between the two of us. The firefighters would determine who was the better baker—and we vowed to torch each other!

We had a friend build a six-by-four-foot toy fire truck so we could attach mini cupcakes covered in shiny red and silver fondant. We made the windows on the truck out of isomalt: it's sugar, but when it dries, it looks like glass. On the side of the truck, we frosted the letters DCFD and put flashing lights on top—it was an amazing presentation.

The next day, we hit the firehouse kitchen for a sisters' baking showdown—twenty-five years in the making! Katherine and one firefighter on one team, making a Banana Split cupcake. Sophie and a second firefighter on the other, doing a Campfire cupcake, which they planned to set on fire with a blow torch (show-offs!). When Sophie went to take her tray of cupcakes out of the oven, the oven was on fire. Apparently, firefighters are too busy saving lives to clean out their ovens. The cupcakes were almost cremated!

When it came time for the judging, we both thought we were the winner, hands down. But the Banana Split cupcake was the unanimous choice—the firefighters said it was messy, just the way they like them. One small victory for little sisters everywhere. . . .

What you didn't see: We got to hang out with all the firefighters for the whole day and it was a lot of fun. Turns out, firefighters *love* cupcakes, and after the bake-off, they stopped by the shop all the time to get more cupcakes!

Banana Split Cupcakes

Makes 12 cupcakes

FOR THE CUPCAKES

1 ¼ cups all-purpose flour

1 ½ teaspoons baking powder

¼ teaspoon salt

½ teaspoon ground cinnamon

½ teaspoon ground nutmeg

8 tablespoons unsalted butter, at room
   temperature

1 cup sugar

2 eggs, at room temperature

1 cup mashed bananas (2 to 3 bananas)

1 tablespoon honey

⅓ cup water

FOR THE CHOCOLATE GANACHE

See recipe, page 69.

FOR THE FROSTING

4 tablespoons unsalted butter, at room
   temperature

6 ounces cream cheese, at room temperature

4 cups confectioners' sugar, sifted

½ teaspoon pure vanilla extract

1 cup chocolate ganache (see recipe, page 69)

¼ cup rainbow sprinkles

¼ cup crumbled toffee

¼ cup toasted hazelnuts

12 maraschino cherries

For the cupcakes:

❶ Preheat the oven to 350°F. Line a standard cupcake pan with twelve paper baking cups, or grease the pan with butter if not using baking cups.

❷ Sift together the flour, baking powder, salt, cinnamon, and nutmeg on a piece of parchment paper or wax paper and set aside.

❸ Cream together butter and sugar for 3 to 5 minutes, or until light and fluffy.

❹ Add the eggs one at a time, mixing slowly after each addition.

5 Add the bananas and honey, and mix slowly until well incorporated.

6 Add one third of the dry ingredients, followed by one third of the water, and mix thoroughly. Repeat. Stop to scrape down the bowl as needed. Add the last third of the dry ingredients, followed by the last third of the water, and mix thoroughly.

7 Using a standard-size ice-cream scoop, scoop batter into the cupcake pan until the cups are two-thirds full, and bake for 16 to 18 minutes (start checking at 15 minutes), or until a toothpick comes out clean. Transfer the pan to a wire rack to cool completely.

8 Using an apple corer, core out the center of each cupcake and fill with warm chocolate ganache. You can squeeze the chocolate ganache from a squeeze bottle.

For the frosting:

Mix together the butter, cream cheese, confectioners' sugar, and vanilla in the bowl of an electric mixer for 3 to 5 minutes, or until light and airy. Scoop the frosting into a piping bag fitted with a large round tip and frost cupcakes with the signature swirl (see page 23). Top with a drizzle of chocolate ganache, rainbow sprinkles, crumbled toffee, toasted hazelnuts, and a maraschino cherry. Enjoy!

Episode: "Sweet Sixteen"

In this episode, we got an order for a sweet-sixteen rock-and-roll themed party. The girls, Spencer and Lindsey, wanted a giant guitar made out of cupcakes. And if that wasn't enough, it had to glow in the dark! We had no idea how we were going to do that. But we had an idea: tonic water makes things glow because it contains quinine. Neither of us had a sweet-sixteen party when we were growing up, so we were living vicariously through the girls. We just had to do this for them!

We poured tonic water in frosting, then went into our office and turned out the lights. Our teeth and eyes glowed, but not the frosting! Back to the drawing board. We did a little more research. We learned that quinine has something called a fluorescent quantum yield—which means it glows in UV light. We thought if we mixed the tonic water with white fondant, it would glow in the dark. Nope. The next thing we tried was soaking coconut flakes in tonic water. They were soggy—but not really glowy. Then we tried adding the tonic water to piping gel and mixing it thoroughly. Piping gel is an edible clear gel that can be used to glue on fondant or provide a shiny glaze. It worked! And we figured it would be perfect because we could pipe onto fondant, the coconut,

whatever we needed. We crossed our fingers and began to build the cupcake guitar, based on an amazing design by one of our employees. It was a nine-foot wooden guitar, covered in cupcakes, and decorated in multicolored icing and fondant.

The girls also asked us to make pizza cupcakes. We don't usually make savory cupcakes, but we couldn't say no to them. So pizza cupcakes it was—three hundred to be exact. The cake part was made from biscuit dough, and they were covered in black olives, mushrooms, and green peppers. Mommy helped by making her special Greek pizza sauce—although we had to keep her from adding anchovies (gross!).

When the guitar was finally ready, we brushed the strings and letters with our glow-in-the dark piping gel formula. At the venue, we had to get it upstairs, assemble it, then carry it back down for the big reveal. We struggled to get the neck of the guitar in place, but it just wasn't going together with the screws. What would we do—serve it in two pieces? So we took a hammer, banged the screws in, and smashed a cupcake in the process. We did a little surgery with some spare frosting and it was ready!

All the kids were gathered downstairs and we passed out the pizza cupcakes on trays. The girls loved them. We said a quick prayer, did a team cheer, then carried the guitar down the stairs. When we turned out the lights—low and behold—it was glowing. We did it! We lit sparklers around the edges, and Spencer and Lindsey were thrilled. They told us, "This is the coolest sweet sixteen we've been to in our lives!" We felt like we were sixteen again, too!

What you didn't see: We partied like rock stars with the girls, dancing up a storm on the dance floor. Yes, we acted like teenagers, but we had a blast!

Glow-in-the-Dark Frosting

4 tablespoons unsalted butter, at room temperature

6 ounces cream cheese, at room temperature

½ teaspoon pure vanilla extract

4 cups confectioners' sugar, sifted

1 cup piping gel (available in the cake-decorating aisle at most craft stores)

1 cup tonic water

❶ Mix the butter, cream cheese, vanilla, and confectioners' sugar in the bowl of a stand mixer or in a bowl with a handheld electric mixer for 3 to 5 minutes, or until light and fluffy.

❷ Frost cupcakes (flavor of your choice) with frosting using the signature swirl method (see page 23). Let frosting set for 5 to 10 minutes.

3 Mix the piping gel and tonic water together in a small bowl. Using a small pastry brush, lightly brush the piping gel–tonic water mixture onto the frosting of the cupcakes.

4 Place cupcakes under a black light and watch them glow!

Episode: "Gorilla Birthday"

In this episode, we had two very special birthday boys to bake for: the two gorilla brothers, Kwami and Kojo, at the National Zoo. They were turning eleven and nine, and it was going to be a huge party with tons of kids in attendance. Our friends built a gorilla-shaped sculpture out of wire, wood, and foam, and we were going to cover

it in twenty-five hundred mini cupcakes. Sophie thought brown or black would be a traditional color to frost them in, but Katherine—who is a self-proclaimed gorilla expert—insisted on bright orange and yellow. She wanted this to be a party gorilla.

While all this was going on, a customer called and asked for two dozen gluten-free cupcakes for a baby shower. Gluten-free cupcakes can't be baked with all-purpose flour because it contains a protein that some people are unable to digest. So we had to clean and sanitize the entire kitchen, the pots and pans and all the utensils, to properly prepare the recipe. We decided to make Chocolate-Chip Lava Fudge, using gluten-free flour—a blend of fava bean flour, tapioca flour, and garbanzo bean flour. The funniest moment: We asked Mommy for a spatula and she brought us a spoonula. But she couldn't pronounce it. She called it a "scratchula" and a "spoonchula."

We made exactly twenty-four cupcakes and they tasted yummy—like Devil's Food cake. Then we realized we made a major boo-boo: we forgot and tasted one of the two dozen! Now there were only twenty-three cupcakes, and that wasn't the order. There was no more batter left, so we had to do another batch. We didn't want to stay up and bake more, but when you make a mistake, you have to suck it up and fix it. We decorated them with fondant buttercream and adorable 3-D ducks. It took a little extra effort and we were tired, but it was great to know that everyone at the shower could enjoy a gluten-free cupcake that tasted as good as a traditional Georgetown Cupcake.

The next day, it was back to gorilla duty. To make the gorilla's face, we worked with our fondant artist to make a mold, and then we filled it with white chocolate.

We frosted the gorilla with the grass piping tip, creating a furry look. At first, we didn't love the color and worried he looked a little too hairy. But you must have faith and trust your instincts. When it was done, it was amazing. We wrote HAPPY BIRTHDAY KWAME AND KOJO in fondant letters, and added a party hat to the gorilla's head and some fondant banana peels by his feet. We brought it to the zoo where the kids went ape over our creation. We also loved seeing Kwame and Kojo get their own cupcakes; the nutritionist at the zoo made some that were safe for them to eat. We had never been to a gorilla birthday bash before—so much fun! Katherine is still talking about it.

What you didn't see: Katherine's nickname happens to be Koko—after the famous gorilla who can communicate with sign language. As a kid, she was fascinated with a documentary on Koko and thought she and the gorilla had a lot in common! Koko is a female lowland gorilla born in 1971, and she has a sign language vocabulary of more than a thousand words. If you want to learn more about Koko, go to koko.org, the Gorilla Foundation.

Gluten-Free Chocolate-Chip Lava Fudge

Makes 12 cupcakes

FOR THE CUPCAKES

1 ¼ cups *gluten-free* flour (can use any blend—rice, tapioca, or fava or garbanzo bean flour)

½ teaspoon baking soda

¼ teaspoon salt

8 tablespoons European-style unsalted butter, at room temperature (Plugrá brand recommended)

1 ¼ cups sugar

2 large eggs, at room temperature

1 ¼ teaspoons pure vanilla extract (preferably Madagascar Bourbon)

1 cup whole milk, at room temperature

½ cup Valrhona cocoa powder, sifted (may substitute another good-quality cocoa powder)

½ cup chocolate chips (Callebaut recommended)

FOR THE GANACHE FILLING
See recipe, page 69.

FOR THE VANILLA CREAM-CHEESE FROSTING
See recipe, page 20.

For the cupcakes:

1 Preheat the oven to 350°F. Line a standard cupcake pan with twelve paper baking cups, or grease the pan with butter if not using baking cups.

2 Sift together the flour, baking soda, and salt on a sheet of parchment paper or wax paper and set aside.

3 Place the butter in the bowl of a stand mixer or in a bowl with a handheld electric mixer. Beat on medium speed until fluffy. Stop to add the sugar; beat on medium speed until well incorporated. Add the eggs one at a time, mixing slowly after each addition.

4 Combine the vanilla extract and milk in a large liquid measuring cup.

5 Reduce the speed to low. Add one third of the flour mixture to the butter mixture, then gradually add one third of the milk mixture, beating until well incorporated. Add another third of the flour mixture, followed by one third of the milk mixture. Stop to scrape down the bowl as needed. Add the remaining flour mixture, followed by the remaining milk mixture, and mix slowly until just combined.

6 Add the cocoa powder, beating on low speed just until incorporated. Fold in the chocolate chips using a spatula.

7 Use a standard-size ice-cream scoop to fill each baking cup with batter, so that the wells are two-thirds full. Bake for 18 to 20 minutes (start checking at 15 minutes), or until a toothpick inserted into the center of a cupcake comes out clean. Transfer the pan to a wire rack to cool completely.

For the ganache:

1 See recipe, page 69. Pour the ganache into a plastic squeeze bottle.

2 After the cupcakes have cooled, poke each cupcake with an apple corer and push it all the way through. Be careful not to rip through the baking cup. Remove the cupcake core.

3 Squeeze chocolate ganache into each cupcake core until you reach the top.

For the frosting:

See recipe, page 20. Frost gluten-free cupcakes with the signature swirl (see page 23). Drizzle ganache on top of each cupcake in a star pattern for an extra-special touch.

Episode: "Shoe-in"

The Drag Race is a huge tradition in DC where men race around three city blocks in high heels. So in this episode, we made a four-foot-tall stiletto display out of cupcakes for the thousands of people who participate and watch the race. We decided to use a PVC pipe for the heel and foam for the base, and then we'd cover the whole shoe with fifteen hundred red fondant-covered mini cupcakes. We steamed the cupcakes to make them look like shiny red patent leather.

While this project was under way, we also decided to have a sisters' cupcake showdown to decide which Halloween cupcake to offer in the shop. Katherine wanted to make the Chocolate Goo-nache (see page 29); Sophie's idea was a trick-or-treat candy cupcake. We let the staff decide—and they picked the Goo-nache (only Mommy voted for Sophie!).

A few of the drag queens dared two of our staff to join the race. So our staff members dressed up like us in drag. They looked so funny, and they loved impersonating us—lipstick, wigs, pink aprons, and all. One was a little upset that the red heels they made him wear clashed with his pink outfit—but he was a trooper, and they had the time of their lives.

What you didn't see: Mommy waved some salt around Katherine to cure her headache, baked a garlic cupcake with a Greek evil eye, and scolded us for putting shoes on a table (very bad luck). But those aren't the only superstitions from her Greek heritage she lectured us about in this episode. For example, you shouldn't cross your legs at the table—that's a major no-no. Or if you enter your house through one door, you have to exit through that same door, or else it's bad luck. Mommy's list goes on and on!

Sophie's Trick-or-Treat Candy Cupcakes

Makes 12 cupcakes

FOR THE CUPCAKES

1 ¼ cups all-purpose flour

½ teaspoon baking soda

¼ teaspoon salt

8 tablespoons European-style unsalted
   butter, at room temperature (Plugrá brand
   recommended)

1 ¼ cups sugar

2 large eggs, at room temperature

1 ¼ teaspoons pure vanilla extract (preferably
   Madagascar Bourbon)

1 cup whole milk, at room temperature

½ cup Valrhona cocoa powder, sifted
   (may substitute another good-quality cocoa
   powder)

FOR THE CARAMEL FILLING

See recipe, page 20.

FOR THE GANACHE FILLING

See recipe, page 69.

FOR THE PEANUT BUTTER FROSTING

4 tablespoons butter, at room temperature

6 ounces cream cheese, at room temperature

½ teaspoon pure vanilla extract

4 cups confectioners' sugar, sifted

½ cup creamy (smooth) peanut butter

FOR THE DECORATIONS

½ cup crushed toffee

8 ounces M&M's candies

For the cupcakes:

1 Preheat the oven to 350°F. Line a standard cupcake pan with twelve paper baking cups, or grease the pan with butter if not using baking cups.

2 Sift together the flour, baking soda, and salt on a sheet of parchment paper or wax paper and set aside.

3 Place the butter in the bowl of a stand mixer or in a bowl with a handheld electric mixer. Beat on medium speed until fluffy. Stop to add the sugar; beat on medium speed until well incorporated. Add the eggs one at a time, mixing slowly after each addition.

4 Combine the vanilla extract and milk in a large liquid measuring cup.

5 Reduce the speed to low. Add one third of the flour mixture to the butter mixture, then gradually add one third of the milk mixture, mixing until well incorporated. Add another third of the flour mixture, followed by one third of the milk mixture. Stop to scrape down the bowl as needed. Add the remaining flour mixture, followed by the remaining milk mixture, and mix slowly until just combined.

6 Add the cocoa powder, mixing (on low speed) just until incorporated.

7 Use a standard-size ice-cream scoop to fill each baking cup with batter, so that the wells are two-thirds full. Bake for 18 to 20 minutes (start checking at 15 minutes) or until a toothpick inserted into the center of a cupcake comes out clean. Transfer the pan to a wire rack to cool completely.

8 After the cupcakes have cooled, poke each cupcake with an apple corer and push it all the way through. Be careful not to rip through the baking cup. Remove the cupcake core.

For the caramel:

Squeeze caramel (see recipe, page 20) into each cupcake core until you reach the top.

For the ganache:

❶ Pour about 1 cup of the ganache into a plastic squeeze bottle (see recipe, page 72). Dip each cupcake into the remaining chocolate ganache.

❷ Cover tops of cupcakes with crushed toffee pieces.

For the peanut butter frosting:

❶ Combine all the ingredients in the bowl of a stand mixer or in a bowl with a hand-held electric mixer and mix on high speed for 3 to 5 minutes, or until light and airy.

❷ Frost the cupcakes with a signature swirl (see page 23) of peanut butter frosting, on top of the toffee and ganache.

❸ Drizzle ganache on top in a spiderweb pattern for an extra-special touch. Add M&M's around the edges of each cupcake and enjoy.

Episode: "Operation Cupcake"

One of the most memorable events for us on the show and in our lives was when the Pentagon gave us the opportunity to send cupcakes to troops serving in Afghanistan. Check out chapter 7 (page 140) for a complete rundown of this episode and a special recipe.

Episode: "Happy Anniversary!"

For Mommy and Daddy's fortieth anniversary, we decided to throw them a big surprise party. Katherine found their wedding album in the basement, and we dug out a great photo to make a portrait of them out of cupcakes. This job was really different, because it hit at the heart; it was probably the most personal project we've ever done. But it was also one of the most complicated: it involved keeping a secret from Mommy, which isn't easy. She's everywhere in the bakery, and there's no escaping her. We told her we were making a secret new flavor that we didn't want her to know about yet. She was a little suspicious. . . . Since Mommy and Daddy met over pancakes, we decided to make a pancake cupcake. Katherine wanted to use bacon and blueberries, but Sophie thought it would smell too much like a diner. So we had a bake-off—while Mommy continued to snoop. When we were ready for our taste test, she walked in, so we agreed to let her try them. Of course, she chose the bacon and maple syrup cupcake because she *loves* bacon! We were working on the grid for the portrait when Mommy showed up at the lab—and almost ruined the whole surprise. We had to send her and Daddy out to make seven "emergency" deliveries for us. The last site was the Greek restaurant where the anniversary party was—so they were actually unknowingly delivering their own cupcakes to the event.

    The party was amazing! We had cousins, aunts, uncles, Sophie's husband, Steve, and Katherine's fiancé, Ben. You should have seen the look on Mommy's and Daddy's face

when they arrived. They were so happy—and in shock. It was a lot of work, but it was so worth it to see their smiles. We feel really blessed to have such wonderful parents.

What you didn't see: All of our serious *DC Cupcakes* fans may have noticed a familiar face in the background at Mommy and Daddy's fortieth anniversary party. Father Steve, the priest at our church, who asked us to do cupcakes for the Greek festival, came to their anniversary party. What you didn't see in the episode was that we bought our parents new gold wedding bands for their anniversary, because each of them had lost their wedding rings over the past forty years. We stuck the gold rings on their hands in the cupcake portrait. Father Steve blessed these rings, in the cupcakes, and our parents took them out of the icing and put them on each other's fingers. Then Father Steve renewed our parents' wedding vows in front of all the guests at the party. It was quite emotional and Mommy even started to tear up. Then, as you saw, we got the party started!

Bacon Blueberry Pancake Cupcakes

Makes 12 cupcakes

FOR THE CUPCAKES

6 slices maple bacon

1 ¾ cups plus 1 teaspoon sugar

2 ½ cups all-purpose flour

½ teaspoon baking powder

¼ teaspoon salt

8 tablespoons unsalted butter, at room
   temperature

2 large eggs, at room temperature

2 ¼ teaspoons pure vanilla extract

seeds from 1 vanilla bean

1 ¼ cups whole milk, at room temperature

½ cup pure maple syrup

½ cup fresh blueberries

FOR THE MAPLE CREAM-CHEESE FROSTING
See recipe, page 36.

For the cupcakes:

❶ Preheat the oven to 350°F. Line a cupcake pan with twelve paper baking cups, or grease the pan with butter if not using baking cups.

❷ Fry the bacon in a frying pan until very crunchy, approximately 5 to 8 minutes on medium heat. Sprinkle 1 teaspoon of the sugar over the crunchy bacon. Remove from heat, strain grease, and chop up into fine bits. Set aside.

❸ Sift together the flour, baking powder, and salt on a piece of parchment paper or wax paper and set aside.

❹ Place the unsalted butter in the bowl of a stand mixer or in a bowl with a handheld electric mixer. Add the remaining sugar; beat on medium speed until well incorporated.

❺ Add the eggs one at a time, mixing slowly after each addition.

6 Combine the vanilla extract, vanilla bean seeds, and milk in a large liquid measuring cup.

7 Reduce the speed to low. Add one third of the flour mixture to the butter mixture, then gradually add one third of the milk mixture, beating until well incorporated. Repeat. Stop to scrape down the bowl as needed. Add the remaining flour mixture, followed by the remaining milk mixture, and mix slowly until just combined.

8 Add the maple syrup and mix slowly until just combined.

9 Using a spatula, gently fold in the bacon bits and the blueberries.

10 Using a standard-size ice-cream scoop, scoop batter into baking cups so they are two-thirds full, and bake for 18 to 20 minutes (start checking at 15 minutes), or until a toothpick inserted into the center of a cupcake comes out clean. Transfer the pan to a wire rack to cool completely.

For the frosting:

See recipe, page 37. Scoop frosting into a piping bag fitted with a large round tip and frost cupcakes with the signature swirl (see page 23). Garnish with a sprinkling of bacon bits!

Episode: "Cupcake Jackpot!"

One of our customers was throwing her husband a surprise fortieth birthday party, and she asked us to make a giant slot machine out of a thousand mini cupcakes to go with the party's casino theme. Mommy pointed out that the slot machine actually had to work. But was that possible? *Wouldn't it be great,* we thought, *if you could pull the handle and different toppings came out?* Steve, Sophie's husband, knows a lot about physics and engineering, so we asked him to help. He was up all night, making it out of wood and

foam, and we sent Mommy shopping to get the materials we needed for the mechanism. She got everything wrong—she bought boot shapers and actually thought they would make a great handle! Poor Steve was forced to wing it. He had all these gears and tubes filled with toppings that were supposed to spin—and it actually worked!

We stood in the back of the truck with the slot machine, amazed that everything had gone so smoothly. Just then, our driver slammed on the breaks, and we heard sirens. We knew it was illegal to make slot machines . . . but one out of cupcakes? One of our staff opened the back of the truck, and the officers peered in. We were holding our breath. One informed us, "This is not a passenger compartment. No one is wearing a seatbelt. . . ." We were terrified and apologized profusely. Turns out, we were not allowed to drive on the street because it is the street the White House is on. We were really shaken up—we kept picturing ourselves in jail and Mommy visiting us. Maybe she could bring us some cupcakes with a file baked in them?

Luckily, the police let us off the hook, and we made it to the event in time. Our slot machine rocked—it was by far the coolest thing we've ever made. People pulled the arm and out came a cupcake covered in rainbow sprinkles. We felt like a pair of winners—when we could have easily been a pair of jailbirds!

What you didn't see: When we got pulled over, the police officer really chewed us out! We were so nervous that we actually pushed the cupcake slot machine around before the police officers opened the door. We didn't want them to see the gears in the back of the slot machine because it looked really fishy. When the police officer asked us what the heck it was, Katherine said it was a slot machine made out of cupcakes. Then she got so nervous that she blurted out that it was functioning, too! Luckily, he just gave us a funny look and didn't slap on the cuffs!

Setting Up a Cupcake-Decorating Bar for a Party!

The fun of creating our cupcake slot machine was that it was interactive and guests could top their cupcakes with a bunch of different toppings. Decorating your own cupcake at the party was a lot of fun. Since building a cupcake slot machine is kind of difficult to do at home, an easy way to make cupcakes the centerpiece of your party is to set up a fun cupcake-decorating bar with a variety of frosting flavors, toppings, and fondant pieces. Then, let the guests frost their own cupcakes and decorate with their choice of fun toppings. Don't be afraid to go wild and crazy with the toppings—you can do anything from chocolate sprinkles to hot fudge, caramel sauce, toffee crumbles, M&Ms, gummy bears, and more!

Episode: "Fashion Victims"

The executive director of DC Fashion Week asked us to make a couture wedding dress . . . out of cupcakes! He wanted his model to be able to walk down the runway wearing it and insisted that it be "perfect." It was for the finale, and he wanted everyone's mouth to drop open when they saw it. We knew we could make art—but wearable art? This was a tall order.

We put Mommy to work measuring the model, since she's an expert seamstress and used to make our clothes when we were little. Meanwhile, we went to the lab to

start experimenting. The dress structure was to consist of a bustier and a duct-tape belt that would hold several swim noodles in place. Then, we would attach four hundred mini cupcakes, decorated with fondant, edible pearls, and flowers. To make a wedding gown out of fabric is a huge challenge, but one out of cupcakes . . . this was the hardest thing we'd ever done. When Katherine tried the cupcake skirt on, it was so heavy, she felt like she was going to fall over. So we gave up on the idea of a model being able to wear it. It would just have to rest on a dress form.

The day of the fashion show, we started to pack up the dress to take it to the venue, and all the cupcakes fell off; everything was literally falling apart at the seams! We had three to four hours to get it ready—and we needed double that amount. The director came by and told us he was very concerned; the display had to be ready by the end of the show. It was terrifying. The music was starting, the fashion show was beginning, and we were piping like mad women! We just made it, and everyone was delighted. This episode was one of the most stressful of all time.

What you didn't see: Almost all the cupcakes that were on the dress fell off in transit. Sophie was so stressed out, she lost her voice—that's why she didn't talk much during the episode. At the end of the fashion show, Katherine actually tried the dress on. Mommy, Steve, and Sophie held the dress up since it weighed close to three hundred pounds with all that buttercream. Katherine took one step and the whole thing fell off her! Talk about fashion roadkill!

Georgetown Cupcake's Chocolate Ganache Cupcakes— Low-Fat Version!

We decided to make low-fat cupcakes for all the people at the fashion show—because we wanted even those figure-conscious models to eat them! In this low-fat version of Georgetown Cupcake's award-winning recipe, a few easy ingredient substitutions knock down the calories and the fat!

Makes 18 cupcakes

FOR THE CUPCAKES
1 ¼ cups all-purpose flour
½ teaspoon baking soda
¼ teaspoon salt
8 tablespoons unsweetened applesauce
1 ¼ cups sugar
2 large eggs, at room temperature

1 ¼ teaspoons pure vanilla extract
1 cup skim milk, at room temperature
½ cup good-quality cocoa powder, sifted

FOR THE FROSTING
2 cups good-quality semisweet chocolate chips

For the cupcakes:

1 Preheat the oven to 350°F. Line a standard cupcake pan with twelve paper baking cups, and a second pan with six baking cups, or grease pans with butter if not using baking cups.

2 Sift together the flour, baking soda, and salt on a sheet of parchment paper or wax paper and set aside.

3 Place the applesauce in the bowl of a stand mixer or in a bowl with a handheld electric mixer. Add the sugar; beat on medium speed until well incorporated.

4 Add the eggs one at a time, mixing slowly after each addition.

5 Combine the vanilla extract and skim milk in a large liquid measuring cup.

6 Reduce the speed to low. Add one third of the flour mixture to the applesauce mixture, then gradually add one third of the milk mixture, beating until well incorporated. Add another third of the flour mixture, followed by one third of the milk mixture. Stop to scrape down the bowl as needed. Add the remaining flour mixture, followed by the remaining milk mixture, and beat just until combined.

7 Add the cocoa powder, beating on low speed just until incorporated.

8 Scoop batter into baking cups and bake for 18 to 20 minutes (start checking at 15 minutes) or until a toothpick inserted into the center of a cupcake comes out clean. Transfer the pan to a wire rack to cool completely.

For the frosting:

1 Fill a medium saucepan with an inch or two of water and place over medium-low heat. Place the chocolate chips in a medium glass bowl over the saucepan and melt the chocolate chips. Stir occasionally until the chips are completely melted.

2 Remove the bowl of melted chocolate from the saucepan; let it cool slightly, for 2 to 3 minutes. Carefully dip each cupcake top in the melted chocolate, making sure the cupcake top gets completely coated.

Episode: "Think Pink"

Katherine came bounding into the bakery carrying a huge bag of pink bras. We were asked to make a 3-D sculpture of a bra for the Susan G. Komen Foundation 3-Day Walk, and she bought lots of lingerie to inspire us. The event is pretty amazing; tens of thousands of women walk sixty miles to raise money for breast cancer research. We also had a personal reason for doing this: we lost our grandmother to cancer.

After we chose a pretty hot-pink bra to use as our model, we went to work on the bra sculpture, forming it out of chicken wire, hula hoops, and foam. The plan was to decorate the giant cups with a thousand mini cupcakes and fondant. We painted the cupcakes with a bit of icing gel and attached circles of stamped fondant to give it a lacy look.

In addition to the giant sculpture, we wanted to make pink cupcakes for all the walkers. We had never done a pink cupcake where the actual cupcake part is pink. Katherine thought the most logical thing to do was to make a rhubarb cupcake; but Sophie wasn't convinced and neither was Andres. So it was time for a bake-off! There were a couple rules: no recipes, and first come, first serve for the ingredients. Unfortunately for Katherine, rhubarb wasn't in season (oh, well!). Instead, she quickly snatched the strawberries and raspberries from the

fridge. Sophie decided to try a puree of prickly pear and pomegranates (and some accidental raspberry vinaigrette thrown in!); and Andres used a vanilla base with raw beets inside and beet juice. We blindfolded Mommy and made her the judge. Her choice? Sophie's tangy cupcake (what else is new?). But we decided to use a few ingredients from each—strawberries and prickly pears—for the final product.

We could barely get the sculpture through the door and into the van, and when we got close to the Washington Monument for the closing ceremonies, there was no parking. So we had to carry this giant bra through the entire National Mall. People were staring at us like we were nuts, and the cupcakes were falling off while we walked. We finally made it to the monument, and Jenné Fromm, the spokesperson for the walk, thought it was "phenomenal." Mommy was moved to tears when she saw the finished bra. She was so proud that we were there to support all the women with breast cancer—and so were we.

What you didn't see: Katherine went totally overboard with the bras. She went to several different stores and bought twenty of them! Everyone in the shop was really uncomfortable when she kept taking more and more out of the bag to show us. Bras in a bakery are a little strange. She literally bought every pink bra she could get her hands on; she even bought one for Mommy, who wore it the day of the event! Now we have enough pink bras to last us a couple hundred years.

Pink Strawberry and Prickly Pear Cupcakes

Makes 12 cupcakes

FOR THE CUPCAKES

2 ½ cups all-purpose flour

2 ½ teaspoons baking powder

¼ teaspoon salt

8 tablespoons unsalted butter, at room
temperature

1 ¾ cups sugar

2 large eggs, at room temperature

2 ¼ teaspoons pure vanilla extract

1 ¼ cups whole milk, at room temperature

1 cup fresh strawberries, pureed in a blender

¼ cup prickly pear juice (squeezed fresh from
3 to 4 prickly pears)

FOR THE VANILLA BUTTERCREAM FROSTING
See recipe, page 133.

For the cupcakes:

❶ Preheat the oven to 350°F. Line a cupcake pan with twelve paper baking cups, or grease the pan with butter if not using baking cups.

❷ Sift together the flour, baking powder, and salt on a sheet of parchment paper or wax paper and set aside.

❸ Cream together the butter and sugar for 3 to 5 minutes, until light and fluffy.

❹ Add the eggs one at a time, mixing slowly after each addition.

❺ Add the vanilla extract.

❻ Slowly add one third of the dry ingredients followed by one third of the milk. Mix slowly, and then add another third of the dry ingredients, followed by one third of the milk. Mix slowly until incorporated. Stop to scrape down the bowl as needed. Finally, add the last third of the dry ingredients, following by the last third of the milk. Mix slowly until fully incorporated.

7 Add the pureed strawberries and prickly pear juice, and mix slowly. Your batter should be a beautiful pink color.

8 Using a standard-size ice-cream scoop, scoop the batter into the cupcake pan and bake for 16 to 18 minutes (start checking at 15 minutes). Transfer the pan to a wire rack to cool completely.

For the frosting:

Top with Georgetown Cupcake's vanilla buttercream frosting (see recipe, page 133) and enjoy!

Episode: "So You Think You Can Lion Dance?"

We were so excited to make a Chinese lion out of cupcakes for the Asian Pacific Cultural Series at the National Aquarium in Baltimore. Andres volunteered to make an Asian-flavored cupcake and headed to Chinatown for inspiration. He bought duck eggs, ginger, pickled radishes, mushrooms, tamarind—all sorts of interesting- (and some weird!) tasting things that he wanted to try using in a cupcake. He decided to blend some tamarind—which is a fruit with a slightly sour taste—into a vanilla base and top it with a sweet tangerine-infused buttercream. We were impressed—it was tangy and really different than anything we'd ever made before.

Meanwhile, we came up with our plan: build the lion skeleton out of wood and steel, cover it in chicken wire and foam, and then decorate it with two thousand bright-colored mini cupcakes. It was mammoth! And for added effect, we'd make confetti shoot out of its head! We had to figure out, of course, how to make that happen—and one thing scared us: the confetti poppers came with a warning: "Contains gunpowder."

And we knew that gunpowder and cupcakes don't mix. So we set Steve on devising a confetti canon and crossed our fingers! It was just compressed air and a remote control, so it sounded a lot safer. We counted down: three . . . two . . . one . . . and hit the button. Nothing happened! So we tried it again, and this time it worked. We just prayed it would do it again when we got to the aquarium.

We finished in the nick of time and got the sculpture to the aquarium. We heard drums and cymbals, and the Chinese lion dancers came out and put on a breathtaking display. At the end, our cannon showered the crowd with red confetti—it was pretty amazing, if we do say so ourselves. Not to mention delicious!

What you didn't see: After the confetti went off in our Chinese lion cupcake creation, the lion dancers taught us how to lion dance. It was so challenging because it took so much coordination and strength to bend your knees and jump up in the air while trying to hold the mask up and pull the lever inside the mask to make the lion's eyes blink! Sophie was the back end of the lion and Katherine was the head. What a workout! When we got home that night, we were still doing the lion dance to the sounds of the drums in our head. It was addictive!

Tamarind Cupcakes with Tangerine Buttercream

Makes 12 cupcakes

FOR THE CUPCAKES
2 ½ cups all-purpose flour
2 ½ teaspoons baking powder
¼ teaspoon salt
8 tablespoons unsalted butter, at room temperature

1 ¾ cups sugar
2 large eggs, at room temperature
2 ¼ teaspoons pure vanilla extract
1 ¼ cups whole milk, at room temperature
flesh from 3 tamarinds (available in international grocery stores)

FOR THE TANGERINE BUTTERCREAM

16 tablespoons unsalted butter, at room
  temperature (European style recommended)
4 cups confectioners' sugar, sifted
1 teaspoon whole milk
⅛ teaspoon salt
¼ cup tangerine juice (squeezed from
  6 tangerines)
zest from 6 tangerines

For the cupcakes:

1 Preheat the oven to 350°F. Line a cupcake pan with twelve paper baking cups, or grease the pan with butter if not using baking cups.

2 Sift together the flour, baking powder, and salt on a sheet of parchment paper or wax paper and set aside.

3 Cream together the butter and sugar for 3 to 5 minutes, until light and fluffy.

4 Add the eggs one at a time, mixing slowly after each addition.

5 Add the vanilla extract.

6 Slowly add one third of the dry ingredients followed by one third of the milk. Mix slowly, and then add another third of the dry ingredients, followed by one third of the milk. Mix slowly until incorporated. Stop to scrape down the bowl as needed. Then add the last third of the dry ingredients, followed by the last third of the milk. Mix slowly until fully incorporated.

7 Add the tamarind pulpy flesh and mix slowly, swirling it into the batter, but not mixing it in completely.

8 Using a standard-size ice-cream scoop, scoop the batter into the cupcake pan and bake for 16 to 18 minutes (start checking at 15 minutes). Transfer the pan to a wire rack to cool completely.

For the frosting:

Add all the ingredients into the bowl of a stand mixer or in a bowl with a handheld electric mixer, and mix on high speed until light and airy. Frost cupcakes with the signature swirl (see page 23) and enjoy!

Episode: "Cookie College"

We got a call from a troop of Girl Scouts asking if we would help them earn their baking badges. We were both Girl Scouts when we were younger and actually *failed* our baking badge because Mommy had us make this really complicated Yule log. This was something really near and dear to us—we wanted to give these girls confidence in the kitchen.

We taught them to let the eggs, milk, and butter come to room temperature, and to measure the ingredients exactly by leveling them off. Then we had them tear off some fresh mint leaves to mix into the batter and garnish the cupcake. These Thin Mint cupcakes turned out perfectly—much better than our Yule log!

Afterward, the troop leader invited us to Cookie College at American University to be the keynote speakers. We said we'd love to speak to the three hundred girls graduating. We wanted to share our experiences and say something meaningful. We also decided to make a giant cupcake badge of a thousand mini cupcakes to present to them after the speech. We asked Andres to make Thin Mint cupcakes to bring to the event, but he saw a business opportunity to sell the Girl Scouts on a new cookie flavor: Peanut Butter, Caramel, Chocolate Pretzel. He created the flavor in cupcake form. We thought it was a little manly looking for a cupcake—like you'd eat this with a beer watching a football game. But Andres was determined, so we said he could bring some to pitch. After all, we're all about the entrepreneurial spirit!

We raced to the university and had to finish the giant badge on site. We didn't even have time to write our speech. The Girl Scouts who had come to our shop helped us cut out and apply the rest of the fondant. They all earned their baking badges for their hard work, and the troop leader presented us with badges, too. Andres asked them to try his flavor; they told him it needed more chocolate and more caramel. It was back to the drawing board! But we know full well that if at first you don't succeed, try, try again. And that's the message we gave the girls that day: it may not be easy, but if you follow your dreams and don't give up, you'll get what you want. Just look at us: at long last, we got our baking badges!

What you didn't see: When we got to the venue at Cookie College, the elevators were out of service. We left the cupcake badge by the elevators and took the stairs up to our setup area. When we came back down to get the badge, it was *missing*! Katherine was convinced we were on the wrong floor, but someone had moved the badge. We went running around the entire building praying that someone didn't discard it. We were worried that the janitor may have thrown it out because we left it in front of the elevators without anyone watching it. We eventually saw some of the Girl Scouts pushing it down a hallway to another set of elevators. They really are so helpful!

Thin Mint Cupcakes

Makes 18 cupcakes

FOR THE CUPCAKES

1 ¼ cups all-purpose flour

½ teaspoon baking soda

¼ teaspoon salt

8 tablespoons European-style unsalted butter, at room temperature (Plugrá brand recommended)

1 ¼ cups sugar

2 large eggs, at room temperature

1 ¼ teaspoons pure vanilla extract (Madagascar Bourbon recommended)

1 cup whole milk, at room temperature

½ cup Valrhona cocoa powder, sifted (may substitute another good-quality cocoa powder)

1 cup crushed Thin Mint cookies (approximately 12 cookies)

½ cup heavy cream

1 cup Callebaut semisweet chocolate
chips (may substitute other good-quality
semisweet chocolate chips)

6 whole fresh mint leaves, plus 18 additional
leaves for serving

1 cup crushed Thin Mint cookies (approximately
12 cookies)

For the cupcakes:

1 Preheat the oven to 350°F. Line a standard cupcake pan with twelve paper baking cups, and a second pan with six baking cups, or grease pans with butter if not using baking cups.

2 Sift together the flour, baking soda, and salt on a sheet of wax paper or parchment paper.

3 Place the butter in the bowl of a stand mixer or in a bowl with a handheld electric mixer. Beat on medium speed until fluffy. Stop to add the sugar; beat on medium speed until well incorporated. Add the eggs one at a time, mixing slowly after each addition.

4 Combine the vanilla extract and milk in a large liquid measuring cup.

5 Reduce the speed to low. Add one third of the flour mixture to the butter mixture, then gradually add one third of the milk mixture, beating until well incorporated. Add another third of the flour mixture, followed by one third of the milk mixture. Stop to scrape down the bowl as needed. Add the remaining flour mixture, followed by the remaining milk mixture, and beat just until combined.

6 Add the cocoa powder, beating on low speed just until incorporated.

7 Using a spatula, fold the crushed Thin Mint cookie crumbs into the batter.

8 Use a standard-size ice-cream scoop to fill each baking cup with batter, so that the wells are two-thirds full. Bake for 18 to 20 minutes (start checking at 15 minutes) or until a toothpick inserted into the center of a cupcake comes out clean. Transfer the pan to a wire rack to cool completely.

For the frosting:

1 Lay a large piece of wax paper on your work surface.

2 Combine the heavy cream, chocolate, and 6 mint leaves in a medium heat-proof bowl. Fill a medium saucepan with an inch or two of water and place over medium-low heat. Place the bowl over the saucepan and let the mixture melt, stirring until it is shiny and smooth.

3 Remove the bowl of chocolate ganache from the saucepan; let it cool slightly, for 2 to 3 minutes. Working with one cupcake at a time, carefully dip each cupcake top in the warm ganache, twisting your wrist as needed to make sure the cupcake top gets completely coated. To prevent drips, quickly turn the cupcake right side up and place on the wax paper. Allow the ganache to set for 5 minutes before proceeding.

4 Cover the tops of each of your cupcakes with your crushed Thin Mint crumbs. Top with a fresh mint leaf for a special garnish and enjoy!

Episode: "Tattoo Twosome"

Andres suggested we make a giant tattoo out of cupcakes for the DC Tattoo Arts Expo. Who says cupcakes can't be "bad ass"? We wanted to make something outside

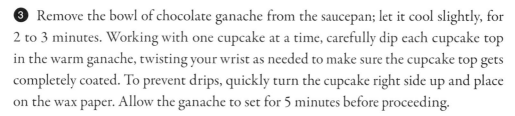

our comfort zone—something edgy and cool. We decided we'd build a plywood base with detachable wings. We'd cupcake it with two thousand minis that we'd frost and airbrush for that tattoo look.

While this was going on, Mommy accidentally spilled coffee on our computer—and it died. Our shipping department had to hand label all the boxes. Having no computer is not an option for us! So we headed out to buy a new one, and left an employee to cupcake the entire tattoo while Andres was baking cupcakes for a bachelorette party.

While we were in Staples, we went a little crazy buying supplies: paper clips, a kitten mouse pad . . . and then we found a pink laptop. A computer in our signature color? Sold! We raced back to continue work on the tattoo. One of us (we couldn't decide who!) forgot to lock the hinge on the back of the sculpture. Of course, it toppled to the floor and all the buttercream was destroyed and had to be redone.

We needed a break, so we decided to check how the bachelorette cupcakes were coming. Andres told us he had done X-rated fondant decorations—and we freaked. But when we opened the box, we found he'd made beautiful little martini glasses on top of the cupcakes. Phew!

At the tattoo expo, we felt like we had a lot to prove—we were afraid people would laugh at us. We wheeled our cupcake tattoo into the room, and there were cheers and applause. Then they started chanting, "Cupcake! Cupcake!" It felt great, because then we knew that cupcakes can appeal to any audience. Like our tattoo said: "Cupcakes rock!"

What you didn't see: We were so distraught when the tattoo sculpture came crashing down and the cameras caught it. We had a major fight afterward about whose fault it really was. But what the cameras didn't catch was that shortly after that meltdown, Katherine accidentally knocked over one of the wings as well! She was rushing by and bumped into the table it was precariously leaning on. That time, there was no doubting who was to blame!

White Chocolate Raspberry Cupcakes

Makes 12 cupcakes

FOR THE CUPCAKES

2 ½ cups all-purpose flour

2 ½ teaspoons baking powder

¼ teaspoon salt

8 tablespoons unsalted butter, at room
temperature

1 ¾ cups sugar

2 large eggs, at room temperature

2 ¼ teaspoons pure vanilla extract

1 ¼ cups whole milk, at room
temperature

½ cup pureed fresh raspberries

½ cup white chocolate chips

FOR THE WHITE CHOCOLATE BUTTERCREAM
FROSTING

½ cup white chocolate chips

16 tablespoons unsalted butter, at room
temperature (European style recommended)

4 cups confectioners' sugar, sifted

1 teaspoon whole milk

⅛ teaspoon salt

For the cupcakes:

1 Preheat the oven to 350°F. Line a cupcake pan with twelve paper baking cups, or grease the pan with butter if not using baking cups.

2 Sift together the flour, baking powder, and salt on a sheet of parchment paper or wax paper and set aside.

3 Cream together the butter and sugar for 3 to 5 minutes, until light and fluffy.

4 Add the eggs one at a time, mixing slowly after each addition.

5 Add the vanilla extract.

6 Slowly add one third of the dry ingredients, followed by one third of the milk. Mix slowly, and then add another third of the dry ingredients, followed by one third of the milk. Mix slowly until incorporated. Stop to scrape down the bowl as needed. Then, add the last third of the dry ingredients, followed by the last third of the milk. Mix slowly until fully incorporated.

7 Add the pureed raspberries and the white chocolate chips and mix slowly.

8 Using a standard-size ice-cream scoop, scoop the batter into the cupcake pan and bake for 16 to 18 minutes (start checking at 15 minutes). Transfer the pan to a wire rack to cool completely.

For the frosting:

Melt the white chocolate chips in a glass bowl over a pot of gently boiling water. Let cool. Add along with the remaining ingredients to the bowl of a stand mixer or to a bowl with a handheld electric mixer, and mix on high speed until light and airy. Frost cupcakes with the signature swirl (see page 23) and enjoy!

Episode: "Katherine's Surprise"

Mommy ran into the bakery and announced to the entire staff and all the customers that Katherine was engaged to Ben—before Katherine could even tell us the news! But Mommy just couldn't contain her excitement. Sophie decided to throw a surprise engagement party, with a giant ring made of cupcakes for the centerpiece. The ring box would be made of wood, the ring itself would be made out of foam, and the entire sculpture would be covered in 2,200 Red Velvet mini cupcakes. The cupcakes would be decorated with buttercream and purple and silver fondant, then the diamond itself would be made from isomalt crystals.

The hardest part: keeping Katherine occupied while we worked on it in the lab. Andres was put on distracting duty! He hid the secret flavor Honey Banana cupcakes and customers were asking for them—so Katherine had to make them all from memory. He was stalling her, trying to make her bake slow, and handing her the wrong ingredients so she had to start all over.

The next day, Sophie made a fake complicated order for Katherine to work on for Leslie, a friend of Ben's. It was a big order to begin with (four dozen!), but it also had a complicated china pattern on it. What she was really doing was making cupcakes for her own engagement party! We told her there was a flood in the lab so no one could help her. She was furious!

After a close call (she tried to get in the lab, but we locked the door), Katherine went to pick up Ben to head over to the party (which they thought was for Leslie.) When they walked in, we all yelled, "Surprise!" She was shocked and really touched. We all toasted the happy couple with champagne and cupcakes.

Katherine's Engagement Cupcakes: Salted Caramel Cupcakes

One of Katherine's all-time favorite cupcakes is Salted Caramel so there were tons of Salted Caramel cupcakes at her engagement party.

Makes 12 cupcakes

FOR THE CUPCAKES

2 ½ cups all-purpose flour

2 ½ teaspoons baking powder

¼ teaspoon salt

8 tablespoons unsalted butter, at room temperature

1 ¾ cups sugar

2 large eggs, at room temperature

2 ¼ teaspoons pure vanilla extract

1 ¼ cups whole milk, at room temperature

1 cup caramel sauce (see recipe, page 20)

FOR THE SALTED CARAMEL BUTTERCREAM

16 tablespoons unsalted butter, at room temperature (European style recommended)

4 cups confectioners' sugar, sifted

1 teaspoon whole milk

1 teaspoon salt

½ cup caramel sauce (see recipe, page 20), plus additional for drizzling on top

For the cupcakes:

1 Preheat the oven to 350°F. Line a cupcake pan with twelve paper baking cups, or grease the pan with butter if not using baking cups.

2 Sift together the flour, baking powder, and salt on a sheet of parchment paper or wax paper and set aside.

3 Cream together the butter and sugar for 3 to 5 minutes, until light and fluffy.

4 Add the eggs one at a time, mixing slowly after each addition.

5 Add the vanilla extract.

6 Slowly add one third of the dry ingredients followed by one third of the milk. Mix slowly, and then add another third of the dry ingredients, followed by one third of the milk. Mix slowly until incorporated. Stop to scrape down the bowl as needed. Then, finally, add the last third of the dry ingredients, followed by the last third of the milk. Mix slowly until fully incorporated.

7 Add the caramel sauce and mix slowly, swirling it into the batter, but not mixing it in completely.

8 Using a standard-size ice-cream scoop, scoop the batter into the cupcake pan and bake for 16 to 18 minutes (start checking at 15 minutes). Transfer the pan to a wire rack to cool completely.

For the frosting:

Add all the ingredients to the bowl of a stand mixer or to a bowl with a handheld electric mixer, and mix on high speed until light and airy. Frost cupcakes with the signature swirl (see page 23), drizzle a caramel flower pattern on top of the cupcakes, and enjoy!

GEORGETOWN CUPCAKE'S EIGHTY FABULOUS FLAVORS (AND COUNTING!)

We do eighteen flavors per day, and they change every day. We add two new seasonal flavors to our menu every month.

1. Apple Cinnamon
2. Banana Chocolate Chip
3. Banana Split
4. Blueberry Cheesecake
5. Blueberry Coffee Cake
6. Boston Crème
7. Campfire Smores
8. Caramel Apple
9. Carrot
10. Cherry Blossom
11. Cherry Cheesecake
12. Chocolate and Vanilla
13. Chocolate Banana
14. Chocolate Birthday
15. Chocolate Chip
16. Chocolate Chocolate Chip
17. Chocolate Coconut
18. Chocolate Cubed
19. Chocolate Eggnog

20. Chocolate Ganache
21. Chocolate Hazelnut
22. Chocolate Key Lime
23. Chocolate Mint
24. Chocolate Orange
25. Chocolate Peanut Butter Chip
26. Chocolate Peanut Butter Swirl
27. Chocolate Peppermint
28. Chocolate Raspberry
29. Chocolate Salted Caramel
30. Chocolate Squared
31. Chocolate Strawberry
32. Chocolate Toffee Crunch
33. Cinnamon
34. Coconut
35. Coconut Key Lime
36. Cookies & Crème
37. German Chocolate
38. Ginger Peach

39. Gingerbread
40. Gluten-Free Lava Fudge
41. Hibiscus Mango
42. Honey Banana
43. Honey Yogurt
44. Hummingbird
45. Irish Crème
46. Key Lime
47. Lava Fudge
48. Lemon Berry
49. Lemon Blossom
50. Lucky Lava Fudge
51. Maple
52. Maple Blueberry
53. Maple Chocolate Chip
54. Milk Chocolate Birthday
55. Milk Chocolate Squared
56. Mint Cookies and Crème
57. Mint Julep
58. Mocha
59. Orange Blossom

60. Peanut Butter Banana
61. Peanut Butter Fudge
62. Pumpkin Spice
63. Red Velvet
64. Salted Caramel
65. Strawberry
66. Strawberry Banana
67. Strawberry Champagne
68. Strawberry Lava Fudge
69. Strawberry Pistachio
70. Tiramisu
71. Toasted Marshmallow
72. Toffee Crunch
73. Triple Berry
74. Vanilla Birthday
75. Vanilla Chocolate
76. Vanilla Hazelnut
77. Vanilla Soy
78. Vanilla Squared
79. White Chocolate Peppermint
80. White Chocolate Raspberry

Utensils and Equipment

1. apple corer
2. baking cups
3. candy thermometer
4. cooling rack
5. cupcake pans
6. graduated glass bowls
7. ice-cream scoops
8. KitchenAid mixer and paddle attachment
9. knife and cutting board
10. large round icing tip
11. liquid measuring cups
12. measuring cups
13. measuring spoons
14. mixing bowls
15. oven mitts
16. oven thermometer
17. pastry bags
18. pastry tips
19. plastic piping bags
20. saucepan
21. sifters
22. spatulas
23. spoonulas
24. squeeze bottle
25. timer
26. zester, grater, or peeler
27. whisks

Ingredients

1. all-purpose flour (King Arthur)
2. apple cider vinegar
3. baking powder
4. baking soda
5. Callebaut chocolate
6. fresh citrus
7. fresh coconut
8. fresh fruits (cherries, strawberries, Gala apples)
9. good pure maple syrup
10. heavy cream
11. molasses
12. peanut butter (Skippy)
13. red food color
14. salt
15. spices (nutmeg, cinnamon, allspice, cloves)
16. sugar
17. unsalted butter (Plugrá)
18. Valrhona cocoa powder
19. vanilla beans
20. vanilla extract (Nielsen-Massey)
21. whole eggs
22. whole milk

CREDITS

· · · · · · · · · · · · ·

INDEX